THE RED BENCH

A DESCENT AND ASCENT INTO MADNESS

JACQUELINE CIOFFA

CONTENTS

FIRST EDITION

ISBN 9781794307193

Independently Published

www.jacquelinecioffa.com

THE RED BENCH, a fantastical, visceral roman à clef follows Cioffa's descent into mental illness and bipolar disorder as she struggles to pick up the pieces of her fractured life after a nervous breakdown. Committed to writing for 365 days she finds solace, hope and strength through a red bench, vivid imagination, the changing seasons and healing power of nature.

"Now pay attention. The next sentence will be the most important words I write. I have loved being alive. I'd like you to pause and remember it as we move through the uncomfortable." – **Jacqueline Cioffa**

PRAISE:

"The magic of Cioffa's work shines its light on the power of the written word." – **Julie Davidow, American Contemporary Artist, co-author of Miami Contemporary Artists**

"I was always impressed by how courageous a writer Jacqueline is. Keep writing your fine prose." – **Mark Blickley, author of THE SACRED MISFITS**

For Laurie Beth

WASHBOARD ABS

I want to dance alone in the dark. I want to hear the underlying music through the deafening mundane silence that is everyday life. I want to make snow angels in a Speedo. I want to smile again without feeling forced. I am going to free myself from the limitations wrapped tightly around my neck. I'm going to discard the heavy and not give it a second thought. I'm going to dance on paper and move mountains with clear thoughts in black and white. The limbo of my life will become a discarded thing of the past. There will be happy, chocolate chip minutes and inviting, familiar scents wafting through stale air.

It will be comfortable.

There will be easy chores, taking out the garbage, doing the jumble, raking fall from the yard. I will bask in delight. I want to live simple. I want orange and red leaves and high school football and small town life. I want to erase the days lived in the hollow and free my mind and body from the trickery of a fast life. I am throwing out the Gucci shoes and Prada bags and the heavy burden and the in crowd.

I will wash away big city, lonely isolation and surround myself with real life. I will turn my back on the superficial and freeze all my assets. I will gladly hand over my stuff and lose pounds in an instant.

I am violently thrashing about. Gently, I am closing a door and cracking open a window.

I am complicated, bruised, and broken enough. The chaos will come along. I want free and easy access. I will no longer add to the misery. My head is rational, my body and soul are saying no more. I hear the words loud and clear, and I make my mark on the paper.

Lose the load and gain the insight. Through the smallest tasks, I'm hopeful. I'll find happy hanging out.

I love it when the clouds swirl and swish about in different directions, knocking angrily against each other in the sky. The clean open sky that I can now lay on the ground and watch free and clear, no city buildings in sight.

I have a new perspective and unobstructed view. I will park my ass on a red, metal bench off in the woods and sit by a pond. I will perform one easy task. I will move my feet back and forth over top of the leaves, balancing back out.

SICK & TIRED

I'm fed up with the shaking in the morning and at night before sleep. The lithium makes me fat, and the fear and paranoia seep through. I'm tired of not owning my thoughts and the rite to a quiet, mundane life. As an artist do I need constant flux to create? How will I find words in the woods surrounded by trees and rotten cornfields? How will I find anything besides dying, wet leaves?

I cannot escape the volume in my head, the constant churning. The Jesus fucking Christ, turn it down chatter. I have been told to be patient. Wait for the drugs, the quieting veil, and the lavender calm to smooth out the ringing. My mind is full of death and black spots I'm sure, much like a stroke patient after a spell.

"The chaos comes with you," simply stated my friend. He was right. I am here, here am I. Sick and tired, tired and bullshit sick. The blank paper waits and my hands navigate the keys and the thoughts go where they may.

. . .

Maybe I'll paint my childhood room the palest shade of grey and modern brown. It will be an adult makeover. I hate the powder blue walls that cover it now; it drums up a false sense of security.

I'm weary of the unrest of the chaotic mind. The half in half out of my life veers to the left or the right as it pleases. I'm disgusted by Reality TV and keeping up with the Jones. I'm disheartened that I once bought into that. I cringe on the subway when I see the city girls and the labels and my desire to spat at them. They are ugly, pathetic and visibly alone; women's lib has not served them well. There is no burly man carrying the heavy high-cost fashion bags and easing the load. I smack myself upside the head as a constant happy reminder of the shallow nothingness I am leaving. Retreat, regroup and rewire.

I would like to not hurl objects towards my mother out of rage and fear, to hate everything around me. The brave face I wear is a façade, hiding the caged animal in survival mode. I do not have one rational thought without an irrational directly behind. I want to die I want to live, I can't seem to make up my mind. I won't live in this indecisive manic depression misery. I have insight into a disease I never asked for. I wish it hadn't left me half –crazed and hyper -aware of precisely what is at stake and lost, and what may or may not be coming. I would like to not plot out an escape route, knowing full well I don't have the courage to follow through.

I would like to wake up a man, ignorant and stupid happy.

I don't want to be disgusted by the fat, lazy, girl on the bus who doesn't offer her seat to the elderly man wobbling about and hanging on above her. Fucking pig. She should be dead not me, and not because of the obesity, because of her unwillingness to see what's right smack in front of her.

. . .

I'm worn down by the façade of things and the superficial. I can no longer keep up. I wear loose fitting cotton clothes; my skin screams uncomfortable and blisters at the touch of expensive designer wares. I'm shopping at Walmart.

I'm embarrassed by the missteps of a life. I see no guiding light. The exotic trips to Rome and Africa and far off places are on hold. The carefree gypsy has lost her way and all roads seem impossible and scary to navigate. The riff raff city and the blah blah noise and the misguided dreams hold no charm. The lackluster and fear have her in a headlock.

It all comes back to a red metal bench in the woods on a small hill by a nothing- special pond. The air is sweet and wet and fall is here for now. Ducks sleep near the brisk, damp water waiting to take flight to sunnier places, offering no solution. I shiver and squirm in my own discomfort, clenching the bench, determined to will myself better. I'll sit there god damn it, you fucking God cocksucker, until there is something to look forward to. I'm as stubborn as you. I'm not pretending rosy and cheery just maybe a hint of enchantment.

I am forced to sit in the unpleasant, unfamiliar silence and hear myself calling. "Lady, so pleased to meet you. Take a load off. You've been running so long. Have the patience and fortitude to be still and walk away from an outdated life. Have the courage to know better. It has been such a long while since you've been home."

I'm going to park my wobbly bobble brain and stubborn ass on that freezing cold bench all winter long chaffing my butt. I'm going to walk for miles and miles through those woods and around that place blistering my toes. I will squash away the crazy.

I'm sick of being tired, and tired of sick. I plan on doing nothing about it.

SPIN CYCLE

The phone rings and I'm immediately brought back to the place of denial. Can you work Friday? Come back to New York for $500 bucks? OH, God, I'm sick and tired and stuck in the middle. Should I go? Run back and grab the dollars? I really need the money. Does the gypsy have one more trip in her? Is she worn out? I'm scared and confused and nothing feels right and my head is playing spin cycle tricks on me.

I'm stuck in the middle between the old, superficial life that doesn't fit and the new that hasn't surfaced. The only constant I have is the vision. The visionary red bench in the woods that says, "Come sit and hang out things will get better."

I love that place, it's the best quiet place to be. It turns down the voices, fills the vacuous empty. On that bench, I control the need to run, I am not screaming inside with doubt. It makes ordinary feel exotic and brings forward only happy memories.

· · ·

Park your butt, sit with the fear and uncertainty and take a stance.

Take charge of your head and fight. Do nothing. Wait. Be honest with yourself; be fair to small town life. Let her wash over your bones and calm the chaos. Stop the hate, sit still and resist the urge to flee. Bite your nails, twist your hair, walk the miles, do the laundry. Double load, double rinse, hang it out, wait for it to dry and work it out. Sit, sit, sit and seize this moment. Change is hard, change is fitting, and change is necessary. No change is limbo revisiting.

People are pulling in all directions. Fuck them; tune 'em out. Figure it out. Trust the page. Let the words guide you. They are yours, for better or worse. Believe in them. They speak your truth.

Your head is screaming, where is the common sense? Dying isn't part of the equation. It's the courageous way out and you are the coward. Your therapist's words keep repeating, there is recovery. Yeah, right! Fucking Betty Crocker, Bette Midler look alike. How the hell would she know? I pretend to be half normal in front of her. I wait, it'll all come out in the wash. Or it won't.

Spin cycle. Repeat rinse, the clothes are dirty, smelly and rotten. Clean up, straighten up your life, and don't think it won't need the fixing.

Remember, quick cash is a cold fix and temporary solution. The real problem is rearranging the wash to a better fit.

RED ROBIN

I fear I don't have the consistency to stay put. The old patterns come creeping in. Run to the red bench and sit I say, before it's too late. Which way is the right way? Which thoughts are going to win? I'm fevered and ill and teetering on shaky ground. I'm tippy -toes with no balance. I'm bound to fall, forward or backward; it's only a matter of time and gravity.

Hatred and fear are winning, crazy washed away clear today.

Run, run, run, NO WAIT, that isn't working. Stay put. Where is the fun? Why can't I escape the worry? Oh, this is putrid. It's worse than maggot filled shit.

I may be well past the point of return. There is nothing back there for me any which way. Pavements are meant for the young to chase, they are better at navigating the uneven.

. . .

The lone red robin of the season takes flight and I open my mouth wide to scream, "WAIT, TAKE ME WITH YOU." My ass is freezing, winter is quickly approaching and my head is whispering, "take off."

A job? Oh god, I would have to be surrounded by people. People are foreign; they speak and move about in tongues and rhythms I don't understand. I see the faces, mother, father, brother, sister, friend. They look like familiar strangers, people I once knew in happier, simpler times. They can't fight this battle for me. Even I don't understand. I am a visitor in my own body, a lost soldier in fields of insanity. If I stay out in the woods, maybe sickness won't find me.

I'm waiting for steady, but steady escapes me. Today I am closing my eyes and becoming the red robin, in all her glorious abundant color. Today I am steadying myself with the positive and the vision.

I am well meaning, yet deeply and disturbingly misunderstood.

APPLE TURNOVER

I want to melt cinder blocks into the bottom of my shoes. I want to slow down the fast, heated pace. I am the fool, out running. Somewhere inside this tick and ache there has to be the calm layer. I look in the mirror, eyes black and blue, circles darker than ever imagined. I don't recognize the person whose mind has been racked and chemically poisoned. I am exhaustion. I could sleep for one hundred years. My head won't let up. It's churning and moving and grumbling and milling about. It's barking at a volume only I can hear. The outside world appears silent, and moves about indifferently.

Will the red bench and her image be strong enough to keep me here? What grand drama am I missing in the big city? The poor, starved, crazy artist life is meant for the young. I'm old enough to know better, having spent a couple decades perfecting the part.

Consequence hangs heavy on my back now. I am middle aged and hunched over. I'm halfway dying, running in place. I am no longer leading by instinct, my gut untrustworthy and misguided. I'll walk the miles; I'll sit on that bench. I'll wait, fortitude and solitude my only weapons. I'll pray to a god who has been loosely absent.

Loose propaganda and superficial are a lost art. No one really does them justice. The unsettling, empty house knows. There is no magic time capsule; there are only the cards you've been dealt.

The cards remain the same; there is only the wash and shuffle.

Red bench pause, sit quietly and wait. I'll bake apple turnovers solely for the scent.

COFFEE BEANS & SIDEWAY DREAMS

Son of a bitch. The only thing making sense is the cup of coffee in front of me. A million thoughts swirl in my head. You need to better prepare yourself for the future; you're ill equipped to handle responsibility. I feel sick to my stomach; a knot closes my throat. What happened to the conviction to sit? Count the birds in the heavens? Five days in, I'm writing nonsense.

This fucking town is dead. I am dead, thrashing and squirming about in midair, a fish caught with a hook in its mouth. The indecisiveness takes over. When can I go? How do I escape? How fast should I run when I've run out of options?

Outside, I hear a lawn mower chewing up leaves and greedily spitting them out. I could put on my boots and rake until I pass out. The task of tiring the physical body is occupational therapy. It soothes the itch and kills time.

. . .

I know that today, I will walk a big circle for miles and miles and push gravel under my feet. I will bury the anxiety and worry deep under my soles. I will eat no sugar, or carbs. I will do yoga and make my body strong, better equipped to deal with miss-fired neurons.

The creative is always pulling me to the right, leaving the left floating in space out of sync. I feel the unsteady balance standing on my feet. I wish I could be dead first, before everyone I love goes before me.

I know in my bones isolation is the best thing for me. The sick parts keep telling me to head for the door, run fast to the hills, burn out. I've played that part; it's overrated and outdated.

I never liked the jibber jabber bullshit of people anyhow. I am perplexed and amused by the 'normal,' productive ones. Am I the failure by society's measure? I don't care, fuck them then. I'm the lucky one. I get to leisurely reexamine my life and drink coffee at 10:00.

I get to use my eyes, ears, fingers, toes, smell and touch. I get to weave the web; I get to tell the story.

The robin is gone; she left her mark. More profound than any old thing, and much better than superficial stuff we collect. I have a bag of discarded childhood shit ready for the Salvation Army.

10:00 am coffee is the necessity when dealing with the pain of looking in the mirror and saying who is that? She looks slightly familiar, but nothing like her old self. How can she resemble any old version when pieces of the puzzle are missing and the face is broken and cracked?

. . .

Get your ass to the bench, feel the cold, write your red truth and have the power to live with indecision.

A two-year-old that has my blood pulsating through her veins bolts in the door and boldly states, "get out, this is my house!" I smile a bit at the audacity of the statement and the two-year-old psyche that knows perfectly well one day it just might be. You realize this is your first authentic, unforced smile and feel warmth wash over your broken heart. There is a glimmer of hope for her, and her future, not yours.

Wittingly, you half smile, aware your future consists of rocky roads and fistfuls of spit and harnessed illusion.

Coffee at 10:00 am and the occasional red robin in flight is the best you can do. Winter is fast approaching. Close the storm windows in this rickety old home and batten down the hatches. Get ready for the deep, deep, dark, impenetrable freeze. I'm turning off my cell phone, getting down to business and back to the basics.

I see my hands move. I write. I no longer choose to follow the masses or the Jones or the riffraff. I'm choosing something different. My truth, the one that sits like acid boils up in my stomach. The uncomfortable truth buries the hatchet with limbo and one can no longer hideout in ordinary. Life is messy enough without all the trappings. I say to hell with consequence and society's sticky standards. Let the cowards buy their freedom in toys and clothes and judgment, its their waste to clean up. Coffee at 10:00 am is perfectly fitting when doing nothing is in season.

PRUNING MAD

I thought the words and thoughts escaped me, but the mind is perpetual movement and the physical change of space the welcome opportunity. Granted it's a backwards return to an old familiar. A place filled with deep sorrow, craziness and rerun memories. It's a half empty house that holds a far away happy, lost together times and sparse family. I'll take it. It suits me better than isolation and the sad exhausted faces in the big city.

We are a people in search of a nation. We lost our tribe, our values, and our rhythm. I don't want to be reminded of the labels stamped on our backs. I don't care about the tube and the lies, the affairs and the misguided wannabe celebrity. I want authentic personality. I want Chagall and his torture and color and art. I want to be moved and inspired by individuality. Call me crazy. Art makes me to want to walk away from the glamorous life. I am convinced I will not find my way out of the dark if I am not prepared to live for a time in the hollows. I'll squirm and slither, giving in to a forgotten town where nothing happens. It's a stand still place where nature is your best bet for entertainment.

. . .

I say bring it on motherfuckers. Throw me more shit to swallow, give me the pills. I'll take the drugs, hand me the rage and I'll run with it. I'll make a goddamn mish mashed masterpiece. I will not hurl things, I will shout through my fingers. This place, this twirling planet is unfit. Burn it, drown it and wipe us out. Eradicate the greed, me included, the ego-driven and self-obsessed. Forgo the fast and over processed. It's a bullshit new millennium.

I am going simple until something shifts.

I bury my distaste in the physical task of cutting back the hedges. Every whack of the saw loosens my muscles and frees my thinking. I trim the grass until the sordid is no longer. I work determined and with purpose, like my ancestors.

I want to dirty my knees and bury the hatchet. I will plant flowers and feel the dead working beside me. Today I will shed no tears, I will not cry out in despair. I will grit my teeth. I will find projects that need doing and complete them. I will listen to the wind and wait. I will thank the sun that I'm still here. There must be a bigger reason.

The repetition and tradition quiets the squalls and rough seas rolling around in my head. What is my purpose? Will I lead a life with meaning? Why doesn't God hear me? Where are the motherfucking signs? What am I supposed to do? Will I survive these worst of times? Do I even want to?

I sit outside on this unusually balmy November afternoon shrugging my shoulders. I wonder if anyone out there feels this pain and doubt with me? I worry where have my dead gone and question why can't I go to with them? Was there ever a point to the borrowed minutes and sweet nothings?

Turning the corner is a matter of opinion. I never made that choice. Everyone leave me the fuck alone please, until I find what's waiting. I want no part of this fast paced, over stimulating, hollow, simply filling the borrowed time mad existence.

LIQUID TREES

Someone asked me why I'm not writing about the cool, odd characters all around me in this strange redneck tootin' town? They think it would be the right exercise. I mulled it over for a second and shook my head in disgust.

I cannot see them. I am out of step with their rhythm. People are not my problem; they escape me. My struggle is internal. The material baggage is loaded and heavy. I must rid myself of the excess, live in tune with the trees, talk to the bush, commune with the squirrels and ducks and deer and dead leaves. I need to get solid. We are 75 percent water, liquid trees.

Humans are thinking movement and disappointment. It is hard to get a grip when there is no pause button. I heard somewhere sages return to nature; go back for enlightenment. I would not presume to be anything other than a soul, searching for truth.

.   .   .

There are only lies in fast living. My body is guiding. The constant itch and scratch won't heal in the city. I go back; I have to make money. I practice deep breathing. Six seconds in, six-second pauses, six seconds out. I continue deep breathing the whole journey, well aware of what the big city has taken. The annoying underlying noise, the vibration and incessant movement, the unspoken, unruly, despair and the melancholy undercurrent.

The twitch and numbness in my face and neck creep back in after two days in the concrete, gray jungle. I hold my breath as I navigate Times Square and the rush of the 6:00 o'clock commute. I feel the anger with every nudge of the shoulder and hear the sigh under every whisper. I coexist in desperation. I recognize the misery, the gray state of living.

I wonder is it me? Or am I them? This is where the work comes in. This is where boundaries must live. I am emptying the body and soul and freeing my mind and running back to the red bench. Sitting and holding on for dear life, I am liquid solid. I choose to store away the unhappy faces, to add characters on my time and wait for happy to grab hold.

I walk miles and miles, and ponder. I dare to envision a future. I summon the courage to visit all the painful parts of my past, and to make peace with the ugly. I must embrace the crazy, for it creates vivid colors and emotions, tap dancing across the page.

November is unusually balmy for this time of year.

SADIE LOVE

Black is the color of the moment; gray is the color of my aura.

I am scared of every little thing; the tossing and turning prove it. My inability to cope with the most basic decisions is a reminder of lost sanity. My life is precarious. The Internet is unavailable to waste the time away, forcing me to stare at the walls and pontificate. I would like to put my head straight through; bang some sense back in.

I did not ask for this. I am alone in mush brain. Today is a day I choose not to live, but to sleep walk the motions. I type forbidden thoughts and words on the page hoping it will erase and release the bad memories. Locked wards, psychotropic drugs and even electric shock cannot cure me. Unsure I have a hand in any of this, I am at the mercy of impulse. The sun is creeping through the drapes; reminding me there is life after dinosaurs and death. The birds are still here millions of years later, and the biting November breeze has circled back. The red bench seems so far off and out of place.

I don't think I have the energy to put on warm clothes and take the walk. I would rather live here with excuses and self-pity. Crawl into bed and cover my head. Left side says, "yes, you are losing this fight, today crazy is winning. Your emotions are mine, not yours."

Right side says, "get busy." Eyes closed and grimacing, she envisions a beach, the sun's warmth and sand between her toes. Right brain hums and walks with music in her ears, savoring the sexy colors on her skin. Orange, pink, golden hues and turquoise greens of the sea seduce her. There is a black and white Jack Russell puppy in her right-sided dreams, wagging its tail and walking beside her faithfully.

Sadie love, a new dog and another chance at happy. I hate this place I'm in, I hate the town of one hundred. I hate my mother for believing I will make it; I hate the denial. I hate my friends for getting on with their lives, purpose and significant others. Ouch, I hate the sting of this same old raggedy Ann pattern thinking.

I am water, 75 percent liquid, I had forgotten. It's malleable, it moves. I am not hate; I am not jealousy. I am the bigger person owning nothing but the dream.

I dress, put on warm clothes, a woolen hat, mittens and hiking boots. I pull the hat down tight over my ears, quieting the static. I will make the trek to the red bench in spite of my present state. I'll walk slowly, head down but determined. My ovaries screaming from stress, my head doing somersaults in place. I cannot seem to quench this thirst, yet I drink the well water, taming the insatiable.

There is too much angst in this one body. I fear I may blow, disappear into nothing. I close my eyes, covering them with my hands descending deeper into black freedom. Ah, there is Sadie lovely, smiling up at me. I am sitting Indian style, toes dug deep in the sand. My face looks healthy and tan, full of freckles, with no hint of gray or dark edges, my body strong and upright. The sky is blue, the sun angled just so and the waves crash gently. Sadie runs to and fro testing the waters, returning right back beside me. I am in love with the slightest possibility.

Right brain slowly squashes out left.

I open my eyes in a trance. I am back on the bench, uncomfortable, frozen yet curious. The trees are barren, the animals in hiding. I hear the wind wooing and soothing, I feel her chill upon my neck and shudder. Dusk has settled and I am goose bump alive, teeth chattering cold, yet surprisingly warm hearted. Left brain back in action, volume turned down to manageable. Right brain still working, ball's back in my court.

SHIFTING CELLS & ABANDON

A chipmunk chases a squirrel across my path and I feel like scurrying away with them, far, far, away and out of this mess.

There are few things I know. The woods are good for me. I hear the babbling brook; the red leaves, the hills work my muscles and the valleys burn my shins teaching me patience. The ground happily soaks up my panic, hate, rage and buries it deep in the earth. My pain and destructive thoughts get lost in the land, and the emotional skin is shed. I'm nothing. I don't mind. I would rather be naked and starving, than lazy and well fed.

The air is crisp and the altitude high. Clarity moves in. Out in the woods, I don't think. I am free from racing thoughts, the overzealous brain wheels constant churning. I walk until empty. This is not a time to be weak, mild mannered or unsteady. This is a time to be determined, to grin and bear the unbearable heavy. Do the work, make the changes and find a joyful skin to live in.

.   .   .

I'm grabbing my coat, my hiking boots, gloves and heading out. High heels no longer the necessity. Designer bags are a bust when babies are starving. Children are poor and healthcare's defeated. We are a greedy group, fat, blissfully ignorant and unhappy.

We are at war. I am at war with my thoughts and outdated ways of thinking. I am insane, but clear thinking. The only way out of the woods is radical change and cellular shifting. I won't perpetuate change. I'm not afraid of being poor. I'm more afraid of being broken, shallow, thoughtless, and ambivalent.

I am no longer following. I set the pace. It's fast, steady, and with purpose. I'm not asking for wealth, just a peaceful way of coexisting. I'm not a drone, a fucking follower of the bullshit corporate existence. I am self-forgiving.

I'm at peace with nature and the animals and back at square one. I'm standing at the top of the mountain, naked, beating my chest. My hair in knots, uncombed, primal, dirty, greasy. I love it. I shake my head violently and twist and twirl in place falling down, dizzy and giddy. I stomp, kicking my feet, hurling, jumping with two- year-old abandon, the earth my trampoline. I pivot, dead in my tracks, and release this forbidden energy. I wave my arms in a circular motion high above my head, snapping my fingers in tune with the higher beat.

Time is free; time is luxury. Reliving is a gift, god is you and me.

DAIRY QUEEN

I've devoured endless books, The Tibetan Book of Living and Dying, The Tao of Health, Sex & Longevity, the Wilde's, the Beckett's and the Eliot's searching. I've gazed at the stars to align my planets. I've burned white sage along the perimeters of my house to keep out the dark and unwanted. I've slept with amethyst under my pillow, seeking calm and center. I've grasped tight to pink quartz holding out for love. I've picked up a rune to map out my course. I've called on the dead to feel better in spirit. I've suffered the fool. I've been one. I've been all wrapped up in myself, crazy, sane, rich, poor and famished in an instant.

But, I've never stayed the course. I'm resolute. I'm firm like desert dirt. No excuses, I want well living. The red bench is simple. It offers no gimmick, no fiery beliefs, no time-aged wisdom. It's five slots and four legs of cold-hearted iron. It exists for sitting pleasure or displeasure as the moods strike. No matter the time of day or state of emotion, it stays planted. On my ass, I am forced to reexamine, no talisman in sight. There are no distractions. No cell phone rings, no emails to answer, no place to run, no excuses to make, no childhood patterns to fix, no horrible past to reexamine.

It's air and breath. It's wet grass and daylight, and standstill motion. It's silent discomfort, knowing full well change is brewing.

Maybe I'll walk a bit and think on it.

WORK IT OUT

I'm stressed. The people around me aren't helping. They are caught up in their melodramas, the pagan rituals and rites. They try to drag me along, but I am unwilling. This time, I refuse to get sucked in. I'll stick to the plan, and stand my ground.

I take a deep breath, turn my back and force my feet to walk away. I roll my eyes and shake my head no. I will not falter. I shoulder on. This trek has a purpose, a new way of thinking and a shot at a fresh start.

I'm selfish, for the time being. I'm not on sabbatical, I am a walkabout reshaping and reshifting. It's gray and drizzling, yet unseasonably warm. I wonder what creatures and fairies await in the woods? I wonder what life lessons I'll learn if I stay open? Today is fucked with all her misgivings. Holidays are depressing. I don't get excited by the trimmings, I get sad nostalgic. I am ridding myself of expectations. To hell with tradition and backwards thinking, screw the niceties. This is serious business, getting back to healthy. I want newborn good health, where the slate is wiped clean.

I don't want nice if it means I am dead walking. I've clawed my way out and can't believe what I'm seeing. Disease and insanity surround me. I hear the ugly thoughts people are thinking. I see the nasty looks under the fake smiles, and am shocked by greed and jealousy. I am not alone in this fucked-up, imperfect world. Defective, superficial society is alive and breathing. I have not lied about who I am. I am not apologizing for my state of being. I have not withheld the truth; no one bothered asking.

I am 75% liquid water; the brain is free floating.

Maybe I got it wrong. I should not harness the mind but move in time with her currents. After all, I can swim. I am a strong swimmer even upstream against raging, ruthless water. It's cold out and there is no lukewarm sea to float freely in, so I settle for the next best thing.

Dreaming, I walkabout.

BURIED IN A BEACH

I chose it all, now I am choosing release. The disease is no longer at the forefront. It cannot be the defining force. The fear that I might actually get better, happy and fixed in this one and only life is terrifying, and far more profound. My vision of my best life has been the same since I was seven.

I envision the beach directly accessible from my modern house, oversize comfy white sofas and the yoga mat thrown casually about. The modern wall of glass windows lets in the sweet, sultry multi-colored stream of steady sunlight. Here in this house I am happy. I am whole. I've known her my whole life. I've always believed she is the perfect place for me. There's a desk off in an airy corner, covered in morning dew and paper promise. It's where I turn words into music, with Sadie love sleeping happily at my feet. There is the faintest hint of music off in the distance. My door is always open for friends and neighbors to drop by. I do not mind, it's no bother, for I have learned to love myself and welcome a bit of company.

I live my best life and am at peace with people. I've studied nature and voiced hard opinions. I've done the work; my mirror is no longer broken. I've taken a long look at myself, and responsibly thrown it out on the wind and trusted the breeze. I'm not quite there. I am far off from my best self, but closer than ever imagined. In this house, the dream is real and more alive than any other reality. I'm willing to fight for it.

I've chosen the quickest route to shed pounds, a new path and new pattern. I walkabout. I believe in the power of change and working hard through transition. I'm not sure I know how to navigate these unfamiliar waters. I'm making no plan and sticking to it. I'm rebutting the negative each time it leeches on. "Oh, I remember you. The sick, tired, poor and consumed with self-hatred. The unworthy person."

I didn't start out like this. I was a goddess, a fearless warrior eager for the unchartered. I was happy at birth, an easy smiley baby, always trusting, overly naïve. I took for granted that kindness was always around me.

I grew up, acquired the hate and problems and stuff and distractions. I do not want to live in any old house with four walls, filled with rules and regulations and misconceptions. I don't want to be shallow, undisciplined, unaware, indecisive and unforgiving. I don't want to be the enabler or the victim. I have not added characters to this story simply because they don't fit. I prefer to stick with the basics, the animals and the trees.

I look out at the sad, pre-conditioned faces and am returned to the lost feelings. I taste the screams building up in my throat, the hurling accusations. I immediately remove myself from the physical tantrums and refuse the same old, same old destructive patterns. I will not curl up in fetal position on the bathroom floor, my sobs drenching the carpet. I practice deep breathing and kind thinking.

I grasp onto the red bench instead, the red robin, the positive forces rewiring my thoughts, as I walk across the page releasing it all.

I don't care if you see the weakest part of me, the ugly truth. I am imperfect, diseased, damaged, abused and pre –conditioned, but so are you. I am aware of my misgivings on the surface. I am face to face with the short temper, the judgment, the fear, the Venetian masks I wear for your fancy. Right now, I am checking out.

I will not allow you to judge me, I will hand you all my unholy on a silver platter.

You may do with me whatever you please. I have mulled it over on a red bench for days and months. I have sat and stirred and worried over nothing. I have worn down the rubber soles on my shoes. I am convinced that certainty is nothing. I am loosing the broken record.

I prefer fearless, fairytale princess young at heart, serene and at home on the beach. In my most perfect, well lived in modern, sea-legged, sturdy home. I am free to roam the deserted beach at sunset, with no timetable in view basking in warmth and color. I am healthy and heart open, delighted to casually wander about.

Ah come on, give me a fucking break. Just when I thought the affirmations, and the walk was working the mind is testing me again. I was plotting my way out of the woods and feeling strong about my convictions. Now I'm forced to run right back in.

A note, a simple communication that reads," Sorry, no thanks not interested in the writing from a publisher," sends me to the ledge.

Have I lost the only thing that moves me, the one thing that is rooted in sanity? Sure, I half-heartedly miss the freedom to move about recklessly, the carefree career, the backpacker's life, the easy cash and instant luxury. I've made my peace with the loss of all that. But, to lose the words and the power behind their meaning, no, no, I can't do that. Oh, no I won't do that. There's no way I can live without that. If I have really lost them forever, then it is on your back, God. You sneaky bastard you put them in my head, made me believe they meant something. You made the keys dance. I'm blaming you for this god-awful mess. I'm saying fuck you; I will dance this dance in spite of your silence or I might slits my wrists instead. Blood trickling down my fingers sounds peaceful and inviting.

Bring the words back with more truth, conviction and power before I am dead. Before I hurt myself, or someone else. Before I return to spewing and spitting rage and nonsense.

I'll place it all on the page, rotten lies and buried truths. Trusting the safe space to carry my burdens. Who cares if no one listens? Who cares if I shoulder the blame? It might be nice though to know I once existed, that my life however tragic made a difference.

I am talking to you God; the audience of one. You gave me this torture of a life, the wild dreams, the abuse, the molestations, the insanity, the brutality, and disease. How I thought I was useless and next to nothing. I deserved the black eyes, bloodied lip and the disgusting, inappropriate touching. You gave me strength and enveloping love too, the all-consuming warmth and starving boxer fighter. You pointed me in the right direction, even when I stubbornly went north instead of south. You showed me the way to the woods, where I could heal and breathe again. You closed my eyes and gave me vision, wild imagination, and the mystic beach to live in when the pain ripped my soul apart. You warmed the sand so I could toast my toes and revel in my most favorite place, basking in the colors and scents, the mysterious and mists off the sea when I was dry drowning.

You created the sun to heal my crooked, unholy black-poisoned heart. You moved the clouds to shadow the fiery missteps, the injustices and misgivings. You built a glass house in my head where I could rest, safe and sound.

Today I don't feel like walking, dreaming, fighting, stressing, listening, talking or any old thing. I feel like crying real tears and drowning my pain with more sorrow. Today the bags under my eyes and ache in my back are demons rising. The self-loathing and hate are high tide enough. Today I write in spite of the fear and insecurity, my insignificant ego. I remain liquid solid, connected to the keys, holding on for dear life and some purpose.

I don't care if no one else gets it, there are no new characters in this piece, it's me against you God against me, and you are loosely present and I am wildly doubting and invisible, sadly mistaken. Seems like as good a place as any to start. Today the walk is circular scary, but to do nothing is far worse.

So damn you, damn it all, damn this life to hell; damn myself for forgetting tomorrow will be different. For forgetting I can be strong.

FROSTBITE LIGHTNING

It snowed last night and I woke up starving. December is here up north, and Christmas lights glisten magically under a blanket of sparkly white. I wonder how the woods will look and feel different. What lessons are there if I'm willing? The frost has cleansed the air, refreshed the ground and detoxed the zealot.

I am awake again and determined. I will not wallow in disease. I will work through it. I did not ask for this life, but am told otherwise by the sages. I meticulously planned it out. I plotted my way down the birthing canal, the perfect time, people and place to visit, the magical good fairies, monkeys on my back, family travails, the mermaid filled oceans to dive deep in, the laugh out loud minutes lived happy, the gladiator wars to wage and the ugly misadventures too. I painstakingly made the blueprint, the horrific, the overwhelming, the bitter cold in my bones, and the cleansing warmth of my heart.

It's you against me God, me against you, in a race against time and space and worry. Where tooth fairy wishes and do-overs are forever gone, lost to polluted H_2O and poisoned oxygen.

With snow covering my feet, brisk air stinging my nostrils, I'm atoms and molecules alive. I am no longer dead walking. For one split second, time stands still and I am in awe. I need no money, no shiny things, no social outings, no fancy restaurants, and no silly distractions. I am grateful for this bitch slap in the mirror. I find comfort in the solitude, the red metal, the gritty truths. Today I need nothing, I can think of needing nothing more. I have the power of imagination, the creative, glorious thinking mind. It's all I've ever wanted, I'm grateful ever more.

If I'm lucky, there is a chance at a new day tomorrow, wherein lies the magic possibility of something bigger than we even dare imagine. The mere fact there is chance is the only beautiful we can hope for.

If I am not grateful, I'm a sore loser and a taker. I had a bad day, so what. Who hasn't? I've lived 15,000 days some grand, others not. Who's to say I have 15,000 more?

AFFORDABLE HOUSING

I don't know where I'm going; I just know I won't go back.

I have left 15,000 days behind me. I am somehow lost again in the big city, on some dirty, rundown subway train after dark. Strangers scatter all about, encircling me. I do not look up; terrified the numbing paranoia will creep in. I am determined, keeping my eyes focused directly on the spot before me. I do not interact; I'm not interested in petty business. I am fighting the battle of my life. Fucking shitty subway prisoner. What the hell am I doing? How did I get back to the void, when will I be free?

December, a bitter unforgiving freeze is the night; the unusually quiet and somber holiday fast approaching. Oh, how I hate this place, these people. Oh, how I hate this time, the wrapped packages, the misguided sense of childhood security, the Santa Claus lies. Can't you see on this train, there is room for only one?

.   .   .

A bum, dirty, old and ugly in rat piss filled clothes appears before me. I try hard not to see him, but am forced to notice his feet, his filthy fungus covered toes. Oh God, it's freezing. He has no shoes, wears no soles. He is the pitiless state we are all in. I cannot bear to look. I might vomit unwilling. No one gives him a glance. I have no money, nothing to offer. I am one miss-fired nerve ending away from his circumstance. He walks the train, empty cup in hand begging for a break, a bit of mercy. Not one person gives him a nod, a kind thought. These filthy, fucking greedy earthly beings, I am no better, kinder, or wiser than them.

I am crazy thinking, yet observant, powerless and well wishing. I see everything, you know, I am not blind. I have eyes, legs, arms and a mouth that moves but can fix nothing. I recognize all too well my reality is not so far from his. Who will love me and put up with the tirades and tantrums when my mother has long gone? Will I wander the streets, shoeless, penniless, mind less in search of a home? Does all this pain and regret matter? Have I made some sort of difference? Will the same old stars in the sky remember me a million years forward? Will they lovingly recall with distant, faint memory I was once here and that he was here, that we co-existed a moment through subway space and time?

I am oblivion, the in between being who has not found one place to call her very own. Tomorrow I will run away, rapidly seeking refuge.

The red bench is waiting. Thank God the red bench is firmly planted to the ground. I will dust off the snow with my fingers letting the cold numb over my bones. I will freeze my brain to forget. I will sit silently, not moving for long, long, long, uncomfortable minutes.

I will be humbled and happy I have boots warming my toes, and fingerless gloves covering my hands. I will not forget the face of the shoeless man who sank my cold icicle heart. I am him; he and I are brothers worthwhile. His is a noble character I willingly add to the story.

Blood thoughts ooze from my orifices, defacing the clean, pristine snow. I am millimeters away from making a very bad choice. I will park it and sit. I will wait until desire washes away worry, until life trumps death.

The red bench is affordable housing, a manageable, modern home fit for the homeless, the gypsy and the wavering soul.

Today I am closing my eyes. I am becoming. Today I am saving my own skin, racing home. The gray skies and the cloud cover suit me. It is the perfect frame for this mind and fitting picture for the day.

The stars are off hiding on some distant far away plane, greedily withholding the twinkle and magic luminosity that is the night.

The afternoon is coming to a close; dark is fast approaching. I am manic tired, cold, frozen stiff veins. I am resolute, merely liquid solid. I do not move from this bench, this sacred place of rest.

I somberly await the return of the starry night and some wise men guided reassurance. I realize it is impossibly hard to be around me, to be around subway man. I am aware. The red bench is pragmatic solitude. It is rent control affordable, perfect housing for one.

The animals and woods don't mind sharing. They go about their business, blissfully full of abandon and free from worry. They work mindlessly, but with a strong sense of purpose.

· · ·

I am calmed by the way of the woods.

PERFECTLY UNHAPPY

My hips tense, my head spinning, thick blood pulsates through constricted veins. I am tired, more tired than ever imagined. I cannot find my way. I can't see the beach. I close my eyes tight wishing for immediate transport to the salt filled bubbly ocean, to Sadie's love's warmth, her nuzzling nose, to my pristine, modern wall of glass, beach home. I can't see my desk where I type red truths, important ones soon forgotten.

Where is my safe house? Am I to return to the woods in the blistering storm? The cold is Alaska freezing, unmanageable, relentless and angry. Hesitant, I venture out. In spite of the arctic cover, I go. I know the oxygen is clear thinking. I must run from this smoke filled house. The walls are covered in ash and dust from decades past.

Two-foot icicles dangle from the roof; the thermal underwear beneath my clothes offers little protection. I grab a bag of salt to coat the driveway, clearing a direct path to the woods. I want the quickest route and soft landing. I fear I need the slow trek to regain perspective. The squirrels hopping above in the branches are laughing. They are toasty in their dinghy fur coats, comfortable in the elements. They playfully jump from tree to tree, wild and free. They taunt my aching body, my sluggish legs move slow and heavy through the thick snow covered trail. I walk in spite of the drug induced lead in my bones, rapid cycling on the downward spiral. It is circular motion. There is no easy way out. Fast walking is not in season and goose-down filled parkas are the necessity.

Holiday cookies bake in the kitchen. I don't care; I can't smell them. They offer no pleasure. I am well aware of this sore loser state of being. I am weak and disabled, uncompromising.

What the fuck is happening? I fight and pound my way on the keys. I must matter; I will not obliterate into nothing. I will stay the course. I will not be defeated. I write, and I walk. I sit, gripping the bench begging the nausea and vertigo stop. Stuck, I ponder rocking back and forth. My fingers and toes frozen, they are not broken and move in a heated pace.

I am still here God, here am I? So fuck off and fuck you. The imagination is alive, well and willing. When does fact become fiction become fact? This story is the closet thing to truth. My crazy makes perfect sense. I blur the lines as I see fit. In my head, twisted inside the mind all is fact, and all fiction. One cannot live without the other. The mystical beach, the practical woods and the safe, secure red bench make the unbearable, almost bearable.

I live on the bench, I am the beach, I am the stars, I am the animals wild and free, I am the woods, I am the little girl with blood running through her veins. My heart beats. I exist. I am present, loosening more and more of the heavy load. I am significant, insignificant.

Some not so far off day, I will be someone's close their eyes, foggy, sweet nothing faded memory. I am 15,000 days plus whatever's left and thousands of words pounded on the keys. If I'm lucky, I will be black and white paper legacy shoved hastily in some drawer in a forgotten attic.

I walk the woods. I coat the sidewalk. I shovel the shit. I work through the mundane. I fake a smile and wish away the holidays so I can get back to dreaming and on with the walkabout.

I am perfectly penniless, perfectly happy to live unhappy in this imperfect time and less than perfect season.

THE MECHANIC

I have not always been this person consumed with death grip, but my mind of late is off-kilter. Some rewiring and faulty wires have left me out of whack. There are days when I think I do not have one ounce of fight left. I can't do the necessary work to stave off the incessant, dark thinking. I'm dried out, cooked, frazzled, kaput. I'm chicken soup full of murky thoughts and loose liquids. I'm heart palpitation anxiety, constant backwards glance over the shoulder paranoia, exhaust pipes fuming.

I wallow in the dark a fraction of a second, savoring the seedy familiar jagged edges. I carry suicide in my back pocket, with tic-tacs, a wrench and a hammer. Like a superhero I leap into the void; choosing to lighten the load for now. I have life- saving tasks at hand. I am retraining the mind to live in the light, on the beach, to feel the sun on my skin despite the ugly, gray, drawn out December after-noons. I wander about to run smoother. In movement, I am better equipped to reel in the emotions, lose the anger, the ego, the pride, and the sabotaging notion. Walking with the red bench as my back-drop, I am a less complicated person. I am full of small promise. I am no longer over-thinking, over-wrought, and insignificant. I am liquid solid, less inclined to anxiety. I am the seasoned mechanic reworking the tiniest parts and metal, tinkering and fine-tuning.

Out in the woods, no one cares. The animals go about their business, barely giving me a second glance. The squirrels' most important task for the day is gathering food to survive the harsh winter.

I'm grateful for that, I am less terrified. It takes the pressure off the day and the emotional rollercoaster ride I have been.

SNOWFLAKE TEETHING

This time, I'm really dying. My kidneys are inflamed, shutting down and about to burst. My teeth are rotting and falling out right onto my pillow. I am anxiety bordering on neurotic, tossing and turning in bed. On the ceiling, there is antiquated, one hundred year old block tiling. As I lie back, trying to shush the incessant noise, I count. I find security in the cracks and peeling, their desperate need of a makeover. I find deep comfort in the repetitive. I count and recount, when finished I start all over again. It allows for free thinking and dreaming.

Out in the streets, our small town is starving. Homes are being foreclosed, boarded up and families disappearing. Auctioned off businesses is the new fad. Small town life is expiring; simple is long forgotten. Debt and give me more have taken hold.

I run screaming back to this place, seeking kind refuge. The easy, breezy childhood town has lost her charm and gone bankrupt. I am not blind. Depression is here, and I am powerless. I choose to count the clouds instead.

. . .

The woods are free. There is no fee and admittance is always open. The bench is shiny red, odd familiar. It is security in an iron blanket, I'm grateful it remains. Precious few go to visit; adventurers and story-tellers have come and gone.

Out there I'm mindful of my present, lost inside the easy minutes.

Snowflakes drift and dance merrily by my window. The surreal, winter wonderland leaves me in a trance, winds blowing in all directions. Each snowflake carries a lost memory, a ride taken, a beach breeze, a granted wish, an ugly secret, a happy day and tragic end, circular deaths pass right on by. Every snow crystal is independent thought, unique and whole, balancing out crazy sad with content.

A chill grabs hold in this drafty, old plaster house. I cover my feet with woolen socks. I pull the blankets tight. I glance at the ceiling and recall thousands of days and minutes. I break free from rapid circular thinking. I count straight. I am the lunatic screaming silent, barely fit for the day. I drift along the keys, relying wholeheartedly on the light touch and tap. I hold on to purpose. Mind present, I wait.

Snowflakes are the luxury. They are new vision, a water element that I love. Out on the path today, the sun glistened and sparkled atop light, airy, diamond faceted snow. The blinding brightness of the silver, white scene set change in motion. I am the freezing cold that I hate, strangely comforted by the fluff of the flakes passing through my fingers. I can't catch them; grab hold. Shrugging, I open my hand and release. A sabbatical means many things. I lose myself and focus hard on the small, true moments and minutes lived.

. . .

I pause and stop dead in my tracks. I take in the blinding beauty in these happily ever after woods; the pretty winter season is crisp, cool fitting. I much prefer the beach. My imagination lacks the power to find proper footing for takeoff, and landing is temporarily grounded by the storm.

I settle for familiar, the woods and the ceiling. I pass the time, I don't mind. I have nothing to do for the moment. I have nothing to do at all. My teeth are rooted deeply in my mouth, my kidneys clean and functioning.

I am indifferent. I am despondent, wet, and misty eyed. Tears fall freely, frozen to my cheeks.

SHARE CROPS

In these worst of times, there is magic. I have never been this unhappy, this broken, this angry, this lost, or this alone. I have not been the lucky person; I have relied heavily upon guts and instinct. I have not chosen the hard work, the heavy lifting. I did not always follow through. Today, I am shackling my feet to the ground. I am rooting them in preservation and self worth. I have lived enough struggles to make a difference. The words give life meaning, courage, and strength. God is a mere celestial being, what can he do? His feet are not planted here. I don't feel like day dreaming today, I feel like doing the work. I'm getting dirty, digging deep. I'm crawling back from insanity, days where knives and death were recurrent themes scrolling through my brain. Run, run, run was the theme of the morning and the last thing I heard at night.

I have an odd premonition kind of feeling, when I look back on these days they will be the ones that count. I am alone in my quest for red truth, my walkabout strictly personal. I am alone, in search for higher truth and meaning, purpose being a key element. I am the soul allowed to live in the woods, on the beach in her dreams. I am allotted the luxury of time that is now. I have no job, no task hanging overhead. Nothing is being asked of me, only to feel better. For the moment I am free to dance upon the page. These are precious days, I'm well aware they will come to an end. I type fast, trying to get out the significance.

I have no clue what tomorrow will bring. I am paralyzed and in awe, the possibilities endless. There are few things I know, and few I've taken for granted. I don't need the stuff. The excess baggage weighs me down. In the woods, I'm free from fancy dressing. I am light years away, a carefree traveler. I don't miss the fashion, the superficial, the high heels and the in crowd. The oxygen and the trees leave me be, to think and to grow.

I do not miss the big city, the rough edges, her waste the time away appeal. I don't want or need to go back. I am ok with the quiet village. The words flow freely on country time. I am stalled in a moment. I am at home, safe with my mother. She is best equipped to deal with the mess that is me. Reassuring the anxiety, paranoia and fear are real, but only temporary. She knows best how to appease and soothe the mercurial temperament. She does not give my crazy wings, she will not allow. She makes sure mine are widespread, while planted firmly on my back.

Family is present and all around. It helps, a little to know I am not alone in the physical. They are powerless to solve this puzzle. The mind has a will all her own. I am strong, willing and able. I am a goddamn, stubborn, dirty, backwoods share cropper holding tight to existence. These are the worst, best of times and I am no quitter.

It is wet and mushy out, the climate in tune with my moods. The snowflakes have melted into ugly mess. Global warming has done a number. The woods are hard to navigate. I take large steps avoiding the swamp puddles. The earth soaks up the wet as fast as she can;

water oozing everywhere, drowning her edges. The damp drizzle covers my face; I wipe my eyes to see clearer. The seasons are out of place. I do not mind. I get along with the change in weather. I sit on the bench in the rain and watch it free fall. Spring and the red robin are a season I look forward.

ANTE UP

The snow is back, the med dosage upped. I am done with this manic life. I am giving up the speed and leaving melodrama behind, in an unmade, unkempt bed. I am no longer the child, but barely an adult. I am drugged, snail slow, in a dizzy, nauseous haze. I see people move, dysfunction all around. I can't breathe in this smoke filled, rigged ruled house. I cannot breathe, but am too cold and tired to walka-bout. I must find my footing. I'm not sweeping the floor, washing the clothes. I'm not taking out the garbage, no small-minded chores. They are not priorities when life or death is at stake.

Give me the motherfucking pills. Up the dose you greedy bastards, it's not your body and certainly not your brain. Take less, no more, no less, add another one, take one away. Stop it please for the love of Christ, I can't think straight. I don't give one fuck how pretty the day is. I have been handed a death sentence. Up the drugs, do it or die. Who cares, I'm frazzled. Everyone needs a hot ray of sunshine. I can't remember the last time I didn't reel in a racing head. A change of pace might be a welcome necessity.

. . .

I don't want to walk. I can't find the bench. I don't care about the bush. Just yesterday, out on the path, deer grazed nearby. I counted six, a family united and bound together. I was envious, the closeness appeal and carefree life. They seemed in tune with the trees. Commerce and trade no influence, they don't exist in nature. I am aware the woods would be the best bet for the day. Not today, not for me, there will be no walking. There will be wallowing.

My family is broken. I don't fit the mundane, dysfunctional picture yet disturbingly here I am. I am half alive, deflated at best. I am the unrealistic, insane dreamer who exists prettier on paper.

In my dreams I am the sane, God loved creature. In my dreams, I am able. In my dreams, there is assured love and mystic beaches to discover. In my dreams, the blood orange sunshine's warmth reminds me of carefree youth and journeys to be discovered.

In my dreams, I am arms raised in triumph blissfully walking the miles. I am right here right now, living harmonious. Right here where good, decent humans like you and I belong. Don't we? The lava boils angry hot, and the path grows more treacherous everyday. On sacred ground, I lose my footing. When did we become mass murderers, the lost generation? When did we forget to notice the majestic beauty of the evergreen, too busy counting calculated currency? In my dreams, kindness prevails and pink petals weep hope as they fall underfoot. I like that pretty pretend picture so much better. In my dreams, a slight chance for redemption waits to be happy. Please, dreams don't fail me now.

Am I allowed to wallow this one day, when faced with a death sentence? We are all dying matter. I will stay in bed, my face numb, tears fly free. On this day I will choke on depression. I will not allow many; I cannot afford them. I have seen others fight harder and longer. I carry their names embedded on the brain. They don't start with shallow, callous or self-pity. They start with light hearted, generous and strong. I crawl deep under the covers, clutching tight to a baby feather pillow held snug against my belly, rooting me in the now. I wait for nightfall. I shut my eyes tight, the room black and quiet the only sound. Sleep is not my friend. The racing thoughts and overzealous mind are out to get me. I hear them one and all; they've been here before. Shut up. Shut the fuck up and get out, I say. Not now.

The strangest thing happens as I focus on deep sleep by deep breathing, my red bench appears. I am there, leaf-dancing, snow blanketing my feet. As if a personal gift from God to me, the persistent sun pierces her way through thick clouds, shines new life on my skin.

All is right with my world. They cannot break me. I am alive and dreaming, dreaming I walkabout.

PARASOL LIVING

I'm pissed. These humans distract me with small minds and stupid chores. I asked for one thing, one small selfish demand, a piece of time uninterrupted. A sabbatical, blessed months to do nothing. To walk, write, recharge, and re-wire. I traded in the big city, the fancy apartment, the lure, the luxe, the independence, the chasing pavements and foreign living, for a place to call home.

December is a bust, cookies to bake, presents to buy, commercial rules to live by, relatives dropping by leaving me doped up exhausted. I steal some me time, a precious hour alone. I grab it greedily to walk through the madness.

Sometimes death seems so exotic, the soft exit, serene and quiet. I imagine no sound, no ringing ears, no silent screams, and no crosses to bear. There are only white beaches with miles and miles of sandy freedom, no timetable in view. I hate them, these people caught up with the menial tasks, distracting me. My head hurts from the new drugs, my legs numb, the physical discomfort screams in every direction. They have no idea the pain I am as the mania wreaks havoc.

It's twenty below, the wind howling and snow is hurling mad. I fear I won't make it to the woods. I have no animal armor, no coat of protection. My skin raw and overexposed by the elements; I freeze in mere seconds. The red bench is covered in snow, invisible to the naked eye. I know the precise spot she is hiding. I know exactly how many steps need to be taken. I am the arctic person, strong yet oddly naïve. I press forward, dropping one article of clothing at a time, mapping my way out in the woods.

I am on my knees, Lord. I am knee-deep naked, in snow and frost buried by the blizzard. I am praying you won't leave me out in the cold. The big city isn't fit for a lost lady; small town is safe, even if drunk in depression. I can't claw my way out of this predicament. I roll my neck trying to loosen the knots, in desperate need of oxygen. I am frozen liquid solid, without air I drown ice.

It's simple. Without the white and black ink and the keys, there will be no neat ending. I won't discover the red bench; find solace in the walk and the woods. I won't be humbled, and mystified by the simplistic, pure beauty that is nature. The red robin will die of starvation. I tap my fingers, magically finding her worms to feed. I give her the woods and the trees and the flight south and safe haven.

Without the black magic and white light of the keys, I die alone utterly forgotten. I am the scantily clad homeless woman, pitiful in broken shoes and smelly undergarments. My teeth have fallen out; my hair is dirty and full of grease. I speak to the sky in tongue. There is no mercy, no one remembers me. No one knows that I was once deeply loved and not abandoned. I am a sight for sore eyes, the ugly uncomfortable crazy you cross the street to avoid.

Without my light love tap on the keys, I wander the streets no family in sight, in search of a name, a home, a new chance, and a fresh beginning.

I weave a different middle, altering the stars in the sky, creating a once in a blue moon life and brightening the course. I conceive an overly abundant well–lived purposeful life, prosperous, healthy, happy and kind. The keyboard my magic carpet to heaven. I am counting on you God, to give the story wings and a proper name. I am awfully alone and scared in silence. Do others suffer like this? Do they bear the unbearable hidden? Do others feel loved, and do they trust it? Do they ask the hard questions, praying on bended knee?

Do you care that I suffer? I care that you do. I add bits and pieces so all might feel love. I share fine, sandy, exotic beaches. I create the salt and sea air, cleansing and detoxing the skin. I caress the fur on the page and recreate the familiar scent of adoring, all- encompassing, unconditional puppy love. I share my beach house, a fantastic, modern, eco-friendly home open to all. Inside, Sadie love will greet you ecstatic, never abandoning your feet. I shake doubt, self –pity, illness and dis-ease right off the page. I live in the dream so I can exist better in this strange place we visit. The visions are more real, heart-felt, life- saving and vital than any bad day.

I share the red bench, my sacred home. I lead the way to the woods and the simple walk. The woods and words are the quest, the sabbatical, a new beginning. They exist harmonious with all the mad seasons. They are not some mystical, faraway carpet ride perfect. They are the very practical earthly places I visit, to clear my head.

. . .

Out there in the wild, there are woods enough. The crazy lady saunters by new Victorian, immaculate, elegant, cascades of golden hair upswept neatly, wearing white sateen gloves and twirling a bold, hot pink polka dot parasol. Admired by all, she is good taste and smart living. She is I from a different time, another season. She is God's perfect creature, present now and a million years ago. Well-liked, she is always greeted by name.

POWDER BLITZ

I keep reminding myself to adapt. Adapt to the drugs, the new life, the ANANTA state of being. Adapt to the now, let the physical tasks take root. I am here, in this place filled with woods and rebirth and dug deep in memory. I am powerless, the powder white snowball gaining speed and tumbling forward, a life already set in motion.

January, the blitz is spellbound. White is the color of the air. It covers every blade; each branch, the trees and the homes, filling the sky a paper white coated, cloud cover mist. It is the color of the day, beautiful angry, stale and frost bitten. I shovel ruthless snow from the drive, a long, painstaking, wet, sticky process. I push digging deep, lifting the shovel high above the drift, arms burning heavy amassing the slush pile.

I never asked to be here, in these backwoods. Yet, here I am, light matter at a meager four percent. The universe, the alternates, the planets, the stars, the life unknown, the minutes and the meaning unaccounted for are the true mystery, dark energy at ninety six percent. These are the best and dark days. They are the now minutes I will miss if I do not stay present.

The faded, long ago memories revisited in sweet remorse. They are the stuffing minutes, the indelible insides I am made of. The do it or die, weak and disabled. I don't want to get sucked up by the superficial, greed or the dollar. It means nothing when you are vying for the soul and the heart happy mind.

Caught up with the in crowd, I won't be granted the lessons, or given the purpose. The red bench will be non-existent, a figment of my over zealous imagination. My truth, gritty, dirty, real, honest and heart pure lives on quiet time, in tune with the simpler existence. I push the snow and discover patience. I wait calmly, optimistic and anxious for spring, the red robin and red bench to reappear. My time is hibernation, so the mind can regenerate, crisp crystal clear atoms and molecular cells alive.

I'm sure if I'm real quiet, I'm confident I'll find my way back, in spite of my gloriously disturbed head, whole and intact. The dream and the reality and the dream are white powder blitz magic. The sorcerer's tale already woven over millions of seasons, filled with wild beasts and heavenly creatures, a mad perfect.

The heavier the snow, the faster I work. My muscles ache, I don't mind. I am frozen; reminded I am alive. It is below freezing, the snow three feet deep. The wind screams, blistering exposed skin. Alaska is a state I won't visit. I am no fan of the cold; I co-exist covered in multi layers. I work the shovel, cursing the ice and the snow. I sweat cold. The resolve to change came easy in balmy November. I was the resolve, the purpose, and the overheated. Right now, I'm too chilled to think. Do I close my eyes and instantly transport myself to a mystic, tropical beach? Dreaming about, should I time travel to an alternate state of being? Or should I complete the task at hand, and rejoice in the physical freedom? Do the work, relive the now and accept the limitations.

The mind squashes incessant worry, the over thinking and uses the body and her heated resources, forging on. With every dig of the shovel, the snow gets heavier, wetter and tougher to manage but my brain is grateful for the hard work. I clear the drive with a smirk, eyes wide open, body frozen, biceps burning, face-ice cold, and heart happy.

I do the practical task for my mother, who is heart and mind solid, but aged in body. I do it, you fucking God, because I can. My mind may wobble and betray me, but my legs are planted strong and my arms willing. I do it for her, because I am alive and co-exist in the moment. I will not be the person weak in substance or character. I will dig deep and search high and low. I will fight for respectable choices. I will live honorably, giving fanciful flight and meaning to this fleeting, temporary, horribly sad and horrifically lovely, infinite being mad existence.

ANANTA in Sanskrit means "without end." I have always known I'm a humble traveler just passing through, holding tight to the undercurrent. I have never taken the sacred journey for granted, in my heart or in my head. The snow, the cold and I will learn to get along. There is crystal clear, powder blue blinding beauty in acceptance.

FUZZY COLORS

I have few dollars but am new wealth awake. I am strong, stronger than ever imagined. I am in the big city, the bouncing ball. I am a goddamn block of iron will, the concrete structure swaying graceful, high above.

So few visit insanity and find their way back. I am back however temporary, and blessed with clear thoughts, alert and listening. I am the keen observer, independent and free to move. I observe the aliens with curiosity, running to and fro in a heated frenzy. I stand silent, studying the odd mannerisms, the quirky behaviors. I'm curious, confused by constant motion, heavy traffic and high velocity. I am not one of them. I am uninterested in fancy glossy things, exaggerated customs, and manicured appearances. I move at an odd quiet pace, the stranger out of step.

I watch the mad rush, people racing upstream. I do not fight the undercurrent. I lay back and float free. I don't try to understand, or ask for the solution. I'm grateful for these precious minutes of clarity. I am life lived in the off percent, traveling between light and dark particles at equal speed. I am at the mercy of the uncharted, my mind the world all her own. I wonder how different am I? Do others process the same; do they duck out and escape when things get over-heated? Do they live inside dreams and feel emotions at the extreme?

I would not want any other life. I would not wish for a different self, a do over of any sort. I'm perfectly happy with the outdated clothes on my back. I've given away the glitzy. The beautiful fight and throws of madness, my pain and fear are the multi color rainbows and bright, off colored dressings of the day. They are my palette, the black abyss, the wishy-washy grey, the spell binding indescribable turquoise green, the soothing rockabilly blue, the blazing hot fire red, the sexy yellow, and the sterling silver razzle dazzle white.

These are the colors that match the fever, the dreams and seasons of a life. They are the vast landscapes that paint the portrait. The shades and scents, the emotions and woods are the light and dark that live in me. The dream is my walkabout, and I am the walking dream. It all fits with equal measure. The empty, lone passenger maps her way towards some semblance of open lavender fields and a peaceful co-existence.

That singular, stop time moment is the purest, inner sense of calm I have felt. The notion that I have everything I could possibly need is clarity enough to fill a lifetime. I don't mind the big city blues, the chaos, the grey monochromes, the bizarre way of life. I don't see the bleak shades; I surround myself with a deep bubble of evergreen, and swim in jaybird blue.

The subway bench is dirty and disgusting, but I dream orange. I smell sweet magnolia in spring. I taste blood orange juice on my frozen fingers. I get through this below freezing day, with thoughts of citrus on the brain.

I am shockingly crystal clear, a perfect periwinkle blue in love with the brain waves of rational. I grab tight to the feeling, the happy go lucky minutes fleeting, black thoughts loom menacingly ahead. I am at the mercy of the colors on the brain. She controls the emotion, the range and the depth, spell binding and bittersweet.

I miss the red bench, the solidity she provides. I am safe there in those woods. It is the simple existence necessary for the mad soul. I close my eyes and envision my back leaned against her, enveloped in a blanket of security. I hold tight to this second, this vision of reason. I don't walk; I don't dare move. I don't speak. I sit erect afraid to awaken. I don't even dare to dream. I type fast before clarity turns fuzzy, before the colors go mute.

My legs start to twitch, anxiety rising up.

JAZZY BLUE

I worry. I worry that without the speed and constant anxiety, I'll lose my edge. The colors go dim, the story fades, the red robin disappears, the music goes silent and the days become one. I wonder. I wonder if my racing head weaves the story, creates the storm, and stirs the witch's brew. I wonder if she sets the speed and the pace, if this midway halt is a new velocity I can get used to.

Am I the instrument merely walking the keys? It has been said how lucky I am, the drugs working their magic. I don't feel lucky, I feel numb. I sleep away half the day; my brain indulges in silence. This new found quiet, the calm buzz is a manageable velocity. It is the troublesome new speed I find myself in.

It's the quiet luxury others take for granted. I can't help but wait, terrified when the shoe will drop, to find myself running, racing, screaming in place again. That is the familiar speed, angst and heat of the day. That is the frenzy I am accustomed to.

Crazy sits dormant, greedy for an exit. Today I don't feel the hot pursuit; I take one full breath without pause. Life feels clear; I am in sharp focus. I am not sure I like this new vision. The faces are focus;

sadness and dis-ease are en vogue. I don't like the new facade, the lost humans I see all around. I walk against the current, treading lightly with each precarious step.

The red bench waits patiently for my return. I welcome the visit; the walk comes natural. The drugs give me sweet clarity, a slow motion Benzo view from my perch. The bright colors fade; the dreams hide out, dormant in the far off corners of the brain. Tucked away in a safe spot they remain, eager for a return and immediate access.

I am scared shitless out of my mind, at the halfway mark. I am not better, far from whole. I am at the mercy of sanity. I am not whole, but no longer fully broken.

I am the halfway person, living the halfway mark. It's the gray state of living someone like me is used to, life at the extremes. It's fitting for the winter blitz and blasé time of year in this cold, stark, dreary farmland county. It's simple, small town living where nothing ever really happens. Nothing ever really happens at all, except the monotony. It is bleak seasonal blues, perfect for a dark day.

I will not lose the words or the poetry. I must stay in tune with the tap and the dance. I remain focused, an extreme athlete in training, preparing myself hard for the course. I dig deep and pull out discipline, steadying myself for the trek. I am the walkabout, circular dreaming and seasonal living par for the course.

I grasp tight to the one thing that keeps me safe, the words and their music. The beach, my parasol queen, the woods, my Sadie love, the homeless visits, the sky's ceiling, the mystical stars, the planets, the red bench and the magic. I will not lose sight of purpose or time, or the luxury. The happy harness days, rooted in romance, chance, infinite wonder and weight that keep me grounded in real time. I hold steadfast to the power of imagination, keeping it safe and far from harm.

They are the precious visions, my muses, and my coping mechanisms in this sad, sad, unholy, unhappy, hollow place. They are the Orion's belt, wondrous, alternate universe possibilities that exist for us all. They are the snow crystals dancing and scurrying out my window, creating a world that is a tad mysterious and just beautiful enough.

Sundays in this cold, gray January state are lonely and dismal. It is the saddest day of all, leaving me a jazzy moody blue, lingering. They are the forgotten; get it together days fit for a brand new family and her children. The lucky bastards who have yet to be broken by life's cruel, harsh reality and unforgiving circumstance.

I worry, but I don't pace. Instead I sit still, questioning every little thing. I am exhausted from the intense speed and relentless pace I have been. I am slowed down to manageable, given another glance.

I'm not sure I like the boring, lukewarm temperatures I'm in. The freedom to see what's directly in front of me is unsettling. The rat race remains unattractive and the characters unappealing. The planet's self-destruct mode, the greed and blind, unaware inhabitants are a focus I can live without. I'll take the splendid red robin, the magical trees, the mystic beach, the endless possibility, the familiar path and the practical walk every time. The elegance of finding your spot, your place and your mind wipes out the insignificant. The red bench remains solid, mindful purpose.

I wear my grandmother's modest sliver of a wedding band wrapped snug around my finger; the constant reminder of a simpler way and humbler, easier time.

TAKE AWAY

I've been given a choice. I'm faced with the opportunity. I am just well enough to go back, to the land of superficial and walk free in the big city. I can't, you see. I could never do that. I am a changed person, forever altered by the crazy I have been, the insane out of her mind speaking in tongue version of me. I see in rainbow colors now. Going back would mean leaving behind all the glorious odd shapes and magical half sizes and spiritual worlds I have visited. The places I have been and the basic lessons I have learned are the happiest existence.

The sabbatical is the walk and the walk is key. I exist better in the woods, moving with ease amongst the squirrels, the birds, and the trees. I am the natural state of being. I've been given a shot, a fresh start. I don't want it; no God, I don't want it at all. Please, don't make me go back.

I don't want to coexist with the rats and the lonely race. I don't need to keep up with the Jones, they make my skin crawl. I wear the same, cozy, cotton clothes every day. I don't care how I look. They don't scratch or itch, they don't tug at my waist. They are practical, keeping me warm and comfortable.

I am the survivor, free to roam, allowed to mull about. I have paid an awful fee. I have been dark, ugly, foreign, mad and made friends with the unknown. I have fought my way back from outer space and alternate realities, dark matter floating endlessly.

I see how the majority lives. Kids dying in the streets, devastation runs amok, earth's temperatures off-key, disaster abounds, the homeless discarded, the invisible caged, wailing migrants. I don't want to be part of the blind percent. I'm awake with a heavy heart. Maybe I should take a happy pill, or drink the cool aid and blur the ugly reality. I will not. I refuse to sugar coat the words so that you might feel better. I'm going to walk hard, bear the burden, work the physical, clear the head, speak raw truth and take stock.

I'm going to walk honest and erect with dignity, drifting off the ledge from time to time. No one gets a pity pass or escapes tragedy. Let me bleed, let me scream injustice, let me cry loud love whenever needed. And then, when I've collected my thoughts and quiet strength, let me fight on and carry the heavy burden for the ones who cannot. Giving thanks to all the people and places I have loved, and especially the ones I have not.

I sit on the red bench, giving her a familiar pat. I thank her for the education, the quiet escape from the hard, heavy, haze-filled days. I thank her for the visit without interrogation or shame. I thank her for the solid ability to stay put and remain sound. I thank my bench, we have made it to the halfway mark, uncertain more days are a given. I thank her for the safety and time to regain composure. I thank her for the days of luxurious silence and time well spent. I tell her, I hope to visit again. I nod my head, mindful of the sheer weight of that statement. Hope. Hope is the driving force. Hope is key to the sabbatical, the underlying current, and the sacred mystery. I am choosing the quiet route, the simple way, the light baggage. I don't feel the need to be weighed down for the inevitable return. I want to be ready and nimble, quick to leave on a moment's notice. I want only to carry away the memories; they will be sufficient baggage enough.

I will keep the dreams breathing, promise and mystic qualities intact. The orange sun and the pink shadow she casts are the mercy and beauty that live on my skin. My modern glass, cozy, white beach house and her transparent wall of windows, my desk with stories piled high and gaining substance are all the romance I need. Sadie love, bouncing about and nuzzling my face is the sweet touch that softens my days and gets me through. The stars and moon are my ceiling, stand still the same moment. I look up, mesmerized. I remember to count. Time is imaginary, forever is now and pixie dust dances, floating and sprinkling the air with just the right hint of what if.

ACID QUEEN

I'm supposed to feel happy. I don't. I'm supposed to feel free. I'm not. I'm supposed to feel something, anything but numb and damaged. The pre-existing condition comes at a lofty price. Even solitude has an expiration date. One cannot sabbatical forever. One is told to grow strong, venture back out, and resume the normal way of living. What if I can't?

I'm stuck in this middle and no one can offer any insight. Do I run, stay or do I go? Do I pretend? Pretend that I fit nicely with the ducks and the colony, lined up neatly in a row? Should I settle for the big city, rat race, and the frenetic, impossible pace? My wheels churn constantly, with little warning. I spin in a panic, trying desperately not to be swallowed whole.

The woods, they are safe and kind. They ask no toll, there is no monetary fee. I could stay here forever, my parasol queen and I. Strolling by, she smiles and greets me by name. She asks how I've been, genuinely concerned with my wellbeing. We are visitors she and I, passing through, walking the same path at different times. She suggests we walk together awhile, in silent unison enjoying all the glorious beauty before us.

We walk away the day in luxury. We leisurely visit the trees and greet the squirrels along the path. We have everything we need, my lady from another time and I. The umbrella provides shade; hunger an earthly nuisance, an afterthought for a lady and her queen. We exist on the dream and the tale. The fable is story enough to keep us satiated and enlightened. She and I are just happy, simple and unburdened by the lofty details.

In our woods, we are not crazy or homeless. We are not ugly, selfish, unkind, or improperly clothed. We are polite beings, we do not beg, we walk proud and elegant. We dress in full regalia, this being our house. Sateen gloves and sweatpants are the split century fashion. No one tells us what to do, who to be. We've figured it out for ourselves, the woods our nature guide. My stomach is sour, and nausea and headache are the deciding factors. I will rise above this earthly annoyance. I'm planning a do nothing escape. I walk the woods; sunshine offers a hint of cellular warmth. Today is the 15,000 plus day. It is the perfect halfway mark filled with atoms and molecules spinning. I am liquid solid, I forget. I don't have to be anxiety, worry or fear. I don't have to be self-doubt. I don't have to feel so much self-hatred and the desire to swallow too many pills, and quieting the incessant buzz in my head, making it stop. Everyone goes dark sooner or later.

A baby bird lies frozen and dead, cocooned in her white, cozy, snow grave crossing my path. I cannot believe what I'm seeing, such sorrow and bottomless sadness. Perhaps that is the natural order of things. She dies, alone without her mother so that I may live. I stop for a second to pause and reflect, grateful for the way of the woods. My Parasol queen has disappeared, leaving me to walk the remainder on my own. She has gone back to a different time, more pleasant place for ladies and queens carrying polka dot parasols, and wearing sateen. A more royal time, I imagine. She and I will meet again when our stars realign. For now, I am left alone, to move forward in this new millennium.

I am alive and writing. The keys tap a rhythm all their own. I love that sound. It grants me the gift of possibility. It creates a life far more fabulous, more grandiose than mine. It lets me walk, amongst queens and dream in alternate universes. It allows me the freedom to observe from a red bench, admiring overwhelming beauty of nature. It creates trustworthy Sadie love, the furball shadow love lying curled up at my feet. I feel a hint of happy, unhindered by rigged rules. Here, I don't care about nonsense routines and pagan rituals.

On the page, I find the robin ample nourishment, astonished by her glorious, vibrant, ruby red. I grant her immediate flight, safe take off and a speedy, springtime return.

In these woods, I am independent and sane. I exist fulfilled, loosening the stereotypes and toxic thinking.

GATEKEEPER

I will not live in fear. I must make her my ally. I will eliminate struggle. I will be the simple person, having been self-tortured long enough. I will not miss exotic voyages or the torn backpack weathered life, beaten down by adventure and travel. I will not be the gypsy, leading a reckless life. I will be concerned with what's in front of me, compassion my closest friend. My head doesn't work like the rest, yet I am no more broken than others. I offer my truths, handing over the paranoia and high stakes. Nothing comes along in the end. I will dig a big, black sinkhole out back. I will watch the earth greedily swallow the wasted days, and the good. The junk pile grows tall, the dirt loose, the discarded devoured, and the wasted time forgotten treasures sunken in place.

This is my life. I am the sole gatekeeper, holding the key. If I choose to dream it away so be it. If I have lost my mind, I'll go back to the start. I've been solitude and misery and watched compassion evaporate into rage. I have suffered ignorant fools long enough, who have no clue what a gift it is to be mind whole and light-hearted. I deserve this sabbatical, this halfway healthy pace.

I found my way out of the woods, and off the red bench. Yet, I'm choosing to remain a while longer in their company. I don't see a more regal place. I see greed and intolerance in the streets, on the outskirts of my village. I have lived amongst the fabulously unsatisfied, the conquistadors. Their self-inflated ego too high a price.

I have been all that, the shallow, bustling, empty soul desperately searching to scratch an itch. There is no margin for error when dealing with the unknown, gray matter, and liquid-solid mind at ninety-six percent. I shrug it off. The relationships, the careers, the fast lane is gone but hardly missed. I am not caught up in the preoccupied silly, shallow thousand days. I'm hoping for more.

I cultivate the imagination and grow my village, nurturing, splendid and kind. I visit the woods often. The oxygen is rich, and the air over-abundant. In these woods there is room for everyone; to grow, to think, to ponder, and to ponder.

Someday, perhaps when I grow too old to remember, I might take the red bench for granted. Not today, not now I won't. Not on this day, this halfway, crucial one. These nothing days are the solid, steel ones that matter. They are the sweet look back upon days and remember. They are the cellular memories that make up a life, that crisscrossing with all others and coming full circle millions of years forwards and back.

I will never forget the price. I change direction towards hope if I am to grow. I create new worlds fit for a queen and her court. I will not lose sight of the mystery, the strength of will, the perseverance, the grit, the unexplainable, unbelievable human effort. The fight and unnerving desire to live at any cost dominate everything else. The breathtaking, enduring, unending light and the power of human love transcend time.

I am limited, I know. I have made peace with that. I have bartered away a bit of sanity, but have been given such lovely horizons. The height and depth of emotions and desire run deep.

I am back at my Mother's house, the luckiest girl. There is love abundant in these cracked and faded, plaster walls. I have been granted a standstill moment, a breakthrough time. The days when I try to jump ahead and imagine the empty, unoccupied home, those are the very, very dark, scariest, worst of all bad days. Love has gone black; the house dies unwanted, and disappears into the sinkhole, crumbling upon her own walls.

I try not to dwell on these future events, the days too hard to carry. Instead, I reach desperately for optimism, and never aging my heart. I still need to believe in Peter Pan, in a safe, happy childhood, unconditional love, and stars that shine brilliantly. Alternate planets filled with lovely, kindred spirits, spin right on by in my direction.

They see me, these alternate friends of mine. They watch my struggle, suffering the day, tossing and turning at night. They know my hard life, the shaking, the noise, the caverns of despair in my brain, and carry it away. They whisper to me when I sleep, don't worry precious person, you can't imagine the unnerving beauty that waits. There is no pain in our heavens, only balanced air. There is no fear; the stars absorb the weight with their light. There are no differences; no child is sick or motherless. The sun shines rainbows on storm cloud rainy days and you are whole, at your very brightest.

Don't worry, don't wonder at all. When you wake, you will remember a hint of our visit. Our prayers and good thoughts will remain ion your skin like sweet, subtle mists in summertime. Go on now; do not give it a second thought. You will move through life with childhood ease long forgotten. You will smell sticky, sweet cotton candy the moment you wake. You will smile, all your senses alert, recognizing a better place of a sort. It's the perfect spot for parasol dreaming, red benches, and kind, happy woods. It's the parallel planet where mothers and fathers and children swim, run and play. It is life deliriously drunk and happy, where puppy dogs' tails wag free.

I don't worry about the pain I have been or the cause. I don't fret on the page over the very real looming possibility of the return to crazy. I choose focus, instead. I have created the perfect scene, the most fitting place to learn and the clearest state. I make moments instead.

The beach goes on for miles and miles; the sea is alive and blazons with bold color. My faith is strong and a flicker of hope is lit. I carry it knotted up inside these bizarre, intricate blue-red veins and rickety bones embedded deep, liquid-solid at perfect room temperature. I would not care if this day were my last. I would die honest. I have made the words my own. I have lived in a perfectly fabulous modern, glass house near the sea, the ocean my sleep machine. I have walked among elegant queens, traveled in time with the homeless, dreamt in ruby red and indigo blue.

Then there is my very real family, the few precious aliens close to me, the most ordinary, extraordinary beings. They are my warriors, alive and breathing beside me, rooting me on in the here and now, slaying the demons. They are the holy, mystic, sacred, strange mysterious and bizarre characters I selfishly keep to myself. They are my purpose, the ones that keep me sustained. They help me move gracefully, staying grounded to the earth. They leave me be, to wander, visit other worlds at my leisure and dream in Kodachrome.

They do not doubt my love, my imperfect self, or my well-meaning soul. They do not see me as broken. They respect my creative mind, praying I will always find the way back. They do not look at me sideways, but straight on unembarrassed. I do not speak about them, because they exist better off the page, whole and intact. They are the driving force behind my life, however inconsequential it will be in one hundred years. I trust with my whole heart, that my time mattered to them. I know I was well worth it, despite the pain and suffering.

I tell the tale, my personal walkabout. I embellish perhaps when the tone gets weighted down and in need of lighter flair. I never lie. I write my red truth as only I can. I weave the odd parts and pieces, mixing up the chapters to better resemble the messy, funny, crazy, weirdo and ugly place we exist. My alternate planets wait anxiously, as I get on with the walkabout. I'm in no hurry. It's just a life, the same as a billion others. I am the gatekeeper only to the one. Always ready for the inevitable, I carry a key tucked deep inside my pocket.

I would love to see the lilacs, lavender flocks and fuchsia peonies in bloom. Spring is right around the corner. May comes soon after. I adore the months that look forward to summer.

The sinkhole is filled in, the earth rotates on its axis to visit the sun, and seedlings lie anxiously waiting inches below the dirt.

CARDBOARD CUT OUTS

I'm not sorry. I'm not sorry at all. I deserve this time to be selfish. I'm taking this midday break from the horrible, fractured person I have been. I will not apologize for your discomfort. These days are mine, a simple matter of opinion. I don't care if we don't view the same landscape. I will not apologize for the how or why way I think. You do not get to see me crying myself to sleep, or curled in a ball on the bathroom floor night sweats soaked in terror and incoherency.

It is my turn, my bird's eye view from a raised bench on a mound of dirt. I like how boring it feels, this easy nurturing balance. I have learned to appreciate the leaves living under my feet and the sun dancing through the trees. I have grown accustomed to the wind. I understand her lonesome, desperate, prolonged howl. I am continued isolation, trying to summon the will to breathe.

The dusk hour is my favorite. I am in touch with all things forbidden, I relate to the blackest black and the somber night. She and I are old friends, hardly new acquaintances. She is the insatiable, mountainous desert, a place where I have not lived but know wholly by memory; every cactus, each tree, every smell, and sound embedded deep in the mind. The déjà vu state of being I have been.

The red bench is my perch, a solid place for contemplation. If others prefer the sparkle and jazzy jazz so be it. Let the noise and chaos be their guide, who am I to question? If Mardi Gras, the dance and shiny beads are their scenes, good for them. I never meant to judge how others work through it. Myself, I can't live with all the noise and the clutter. It no longer fits the world I inhabit.

My dance is a subtler tune, flare and fashion discarded long ago, tossed out with foolish accessories. There are enough characters dancing in my head to fill a book. I won't add to the confusion. I no longer have that luxury. Off balance steps and misplaced heels are the extravagances I can live without. Unsteady footing holds lethal consequence when dealing with a mine trap head.

This is walkabout as I see fit. I'm sick and tired of the judgment, how black or white it may look. Have you ever turned your back on someone talking in tongue, like me? I have. I can't lose sleep over uneducated opinions. They don't matter at all to the trees and the squirrels; the red robin shrugs off the insignificant, silly sense of pretense, reminding me to stay the course. Stay focused on the big picture, the circular pattern at the halfway benchmark.

Keep your eyes alert, your ears keen, your heart open and your senses heightened. The purpose is the delicate humility and grace brought to the dance. Those are very real, valid points to be concerned with. Did I care enough? Was I kind enough, even on crazy haze-filled, mad hatter days when I was not quite myself? Did I say thank you often, remembering life is a fleeting sliver of time and small matter? Did I will away the ugly, with thoughts of citrus dancing on the brain? Did I remember to return to the dream, while living the awakened life?

It comes down to the simplest thing, the easy person. Was I kind enough, even on my worst, ugly days filled with blood oozing pain and crazy fear leaking from my orifices? Did I maintain composure while disabled?

Fuck the fear, the constant aggravation, the high school desire to fit in. It's wasted energy. I did not start this journey for another.

I have not come this far, worked this hard and been this determined to waver now. I have chosen the higher purpose, the dream created for one. I have built fantastical mind beaches and hot, orange-yellow sun existence, puppies running about. I have created the sleekest modern, wall of glass beach home and lived by the sea. I've dreamt up the prettiest life, with plenty of reason.

The walk brings along hope, puts a smile on my face and makes sense of the endless matter. I am the wanderer, propelling forward towards the sun. I am hoping the visions remain clear and dream viable, that reality gets washed out to sea and makes room for the tiniest parts of life best suited for me.

I am certain I am in the right place on paper, the perfect order. I don't care about the others, the odd characters or the high and mighty judges. I am quite capable of holding tight to the keys. I am a good person, however flawed. I am the God loving and hating soul, the believer in something better and the bigger picture just inches out of reach. I am equal parts crazy, in love with the dark and the night. I walk free out there on my own, the stars and the wild, infinite sky my freedom backdrop. I am sane enough to fret about perception. I am crazy enough to want to live naked, imperfectly, perfect and exposed by the light.

I don't fear the dark, the judgment or the impossible, alternate worlds I live. In my dreams, there is endless possibility and more than enough room to grow. The red bench is rooted here in real-time, yet holds the sweetest spot in fantasy. She is my go-to place, the central balance where all things swing back to neutral. Gravity is a mere nuisance, the earthly inconvenience she has grown to know.

If she can be regal, then so can I. All things must return to zero. It is the natural order of life. It is the weight of the world we are gifted, borrowing time for 525,600 minutes. I am not fighting the checks and balances. I am evening out the scales and dumping some weight. Circular living and seasonal living makes letting go easy, I need not be reminded. I have been through all kinds of hell and manic lunar phases.

I have been the parasol lady, high Victorian gliding past with nothing to do except admire her path, the polka dot umbrella shading the way. I have been the ugly, poor, crazy homeless woman wandering the streets, the uncomfortable, lost soul you cringe to avoid. God has made me messy, full of awful flaws and heart defects.

At times, I have been the beauty, a statuesque creature envied and admired by all, madness lurking dangerously below the surface, clawing and bursting for a way out. I have been the rustic, city girl too begging for relief, a quiet refuge from my brewing storm. I have been all of that, and more. Fighting, squashing and pleading with the symphony of voices in my head I have been mostly tired, more exhausted asleep than awake.

I do not apologize. No, I won't do that. I can't be sorry for the words or the negative thoughts or the hallucinations, for then the story loses substance. I trust the page to show me how to navigate, with a bit of humor. I am counting on that. I'm a foreigner visiting a blue planet. I can't speak for others; I can put only one house in order. I toss out the things that don't matter. With a sense of duty, I cling to the page.

I love the woods and the bench when all else has gone haywire. I hold tight to the solid image. The shimmery, red velvet bench is the perfect Valentine's place to be in. Sweet February chocolate, and first love. I start there, back at the beginning. Forgive me while I am learning to walk. I am new at this. I'm the toddler, unsteady on her feet, but determined.

I am the walkabout, treading lightly and moving forward the only way I know how.

BROWN BOW

I am unable to release the person I have been. She does not fit this new skin. I ran for so long, it's hard to slow down. I know which decisions I must make to survive. Stubbornly, I continue to test the murky waters.

The city swamp is not where I wish to be, though I choose to swim in the thrashing waters. The big city is not good for a person like me, but stubbornly I return. How can I trust this mind, pushing me in different directions when she is the untrustworthy source? She doesn't mean well, she's the devastating consequence. She's impulse and indecision at it's very best.

Should I trust my shoulders and bunched up neck in knots? Do I trust the breath that gets stuck in my gut and festers acid? Do I pay attention to the numbness creeping up tingling my muscles? Do I race towards the station and board the next bus? Do I get out of dodge, and back to small town living? Do I wait? Do I die, plum out of luck? Do I wait my turn for the inevitable, paralyzed by life and unable to venture out?

I tell myself no that can't be, just stop. Think about it, and be sensible. The red bench is your anchor, the steady guide. She's waiting in those backwoods you know so well. You are strong, you are mighty, you are not only sick. You are bound to this earth temporarily, determined to stay put. You carry stability locked deep in your gut. You gave your word, however sick and disabled.

I am not well today, on this ugly, wet, snow blistering slushy day in February. I am the master of deception, flashing the easy, breezy smile and confident glance. I am not sure anyone really understands the lost mind concept, the unwell I have been. I have not been the comfortable person. Each day I die, my healthy mind disappearing into the abyss. Each time she recedes into the dark, inside the hidden corners of my head, those pieces of me are lost forever.

I will mourn them, my healthy, clear thinking minutes. I drum up the energy and the courage, even without those critical parts. I am nothing, if not the walkabout. I am the walk and the woods and the desire to outsmart my motherfucking crazy, cunning head.

I never asked for this horrible halfway mark, yet here I am. I want to close my eyes and forget. Be nothing, I want to live enveloped in healing jade. I want to sleep for a thousand years, no more racing thoughts, no more rapid cycling. No more dancing demons, no devils floating in the brain. I want the red robin and the sun and hot beaches. I want to surf waves of rational. I must get back on the bus, and return to nature. I must get back to the dream. The dream might save me. There is the slightest sliver of chance.

. . .

My body has slowed down to sluggish, so the mind can rest. I'm alone. I'm completely and utterly alone, keeping company all by myself. There is not one person on this entire, blue people planet that fully understands the battles within. I'm swollen sad, unusually out of place. I'm defeated in spite of my best efforts. I don't think I will make the full go-round, circular living may be the pipedream out of reach.

I can't imagine another halfway mark lived quite like this. Just when I think I have a hold on the dark and the dread, anxiety puts me back in my place. The mad living swells up and starts all over again. Ah, but I hold a secret. The red bench is the place crazy is not allowed to visit. It is the blue safety zone; no ugly, irrational thoughts allowed. I will not let her in my woods, this vampire mind. I own this neutral territory. I am in charge. I am liquid solid, changing form and shape-shifting with the seasons. I will shoo her away and beat her down every single time she tries to get back in. The bitch will be put in her place. I am the hunter, vigilant and ever ready for the kill, blood bow and arrow drawn.

I realize the most peculiar thing; I am fighting with myself. How unbelievably strange it is when your own mind betrays you?

If I had not lived this waking dream, I would be the biggest skeptic. Yet, here I am proof that alternate worlds do in fact exist.

They live hiding in the rafters, in the vicious, angry, high tide swells and dwell in enticing trap doors that taste of blueberry color. There is a modem of decorum to how one walks through it. Insanity, that is. There is no science fiction fix alive in the modern age of science. Technology stops humans from thinking for themselves, writing love letters, over entertained and over preoccupied. Modern times have obliterated art. They don't want you to think for yourself, keeping you preoccupied with electronics. They're excited by the control concept, creating a nation of drones. Soon enough we'll all be wearing uniforms in stiff purple.

Not me man, no thanks. I'll take my brand of crazy over modern culture any day. There are queens and crazies, and frivolous folly holding court. Rapid cycling and dreaming are in season. Fantasy has found her way back home.

AFTERSHOCKS

I put on an aria and hum to forget. Keeping the emptiness at bay a while, I live inside the variations. It feels good, I can relate. I'm awkward tics, squirms, and squishes. I turn down the music, pretending to be normal. The aftershocks. On a gurney hooked to wires in a stale, sterilized hospital room I hear voices and bustling while a pretty blond in scrubs smiles as she places a mask over my face. Soon, I won't remember the delusions losing bits and pieces of memory. I am the aftershock, waiting for the brain waves to settle in.

I plant a bulb inside my house, so I might get a jump on spring. The melting icicles and gray, sunless days have endured winter that has dragged on far too long. It has not helped my state of being. I push through regardless, relying on one thing. The pitter, patter type and the melody of the keys. The red bench lives there, in that familiar sound. The words are in the thousands now, much like my days. The reality and the story are in perfect sync.

I'm hoping I can just stick to the task at hand, and finish what I've set out to do. If I live this sabbatical to it's fullest and write honest, you and I will be in a very good place. We are alive and fulfilled, living free off the page.

On this more than 18,000 words and 15,000 days halfway mark, I make this promise. No matter what, I continue. I hold sacred the walkabout, clinging to the power of transformation. I won't give up God, you greedy bastard. You can't have all of me. Did you hear that? I won't give in to the horrible reality. I won't pay the irrational thoughts any mind. You put them there for a reason, perhaps an ugly debt went unpaid being collected.

I choose to dream in color instead, raspberry and pink quartz quenching my thirst. I am insatiable, I will not be afraid of my eccentric qualities. I will not tone down my mood so others feel ordinary. I embrace them, these mad colors; they must have their place.

You planted the blossoms and garden in my head. I painstakingly cure the roots and the stems, waiting anxiously for the buds to be in bloom. The woods and the walk are different now. Nature has shifted from the dormant freeze. There is the slightest hint of change in the air under the frozen waters. If I close my eyes and take a deep cleansing breath, I smell life waiting.

I look forward to that. March is the month I was born; she and I are old friends loving the spring. I jump ahead of myself. I dream of oceans and salty cleansing waters, the intoxicating cure. The skin sheds winter, the sun warms the bones, and worry passes over the sand on my toes. I anticipate the seasons.

. . .

I have only to look out the window to know winter is not gone. I feel like daydreaming and jumping through time. The alternate planets are alive and well, spinning parallel with my universe. Sadie love frolics on the waves in our sea, a perfect God creature absent from worry. She is sopping, stinky wet and running, flying straight from the earth into my arms. She smells just like the ocean, her hair coarse from the salt water.

I dare to feel laughter as it grows in me. For an instant, on this alternate plane, I forget.

I know this daydream well; we are on familiar terms. I know every crevice and speck of light in the sand, the sultry colors of my ocean, the modern wall of glass home is my perfect backdrop.

I have lived this life before, this waking dream inches from reality.

I catch a glimpse of my reflection in the mirror. I look not like myself at all. I am bloated, out of shape, much older now than at the beginning. I would like to give back some gut-wrenching, too hard thousand days and bury them deep in the dirt. I stand naked above the soil, slicing a tiny cut in my chest in sacrifice so that my heavy heart drips blood satisfying the earth, growing fertile again.

I can't give away only the ugly parts. That is unfair trade, there will be left an unbalance. It's a silly notion, this pagan sacrifice.

I believe in the gods and deities who walked before me.

I have seen them along my way. Some, I have even called by name. They never left me alone in the dark or lost out in my woods. They have been splendid company through the maze. I do hope they won't disappear completely, as I grow strong. I would miss them terribly during the mundane, drawn-out days.

I turn the aria up loud, reverberating the walls and my bones. I close my eyes, sinking deep into an ancient rite and traditional song, savoring the mad genius' that came before. Tears well up as I raise my arms and twirl around. Humming under my breath, I relish the haunting sound.

February it's best to stay indoors, dreaming golden variations. It's a do-nothing month, except planting the seeds for spring.

3:33 PM & GOLDBERG VARIATIONS

Dusk is quick to settle on these deep, tree-filled backwoods deprived of any light. The winter night is closing in; I look forward to it. The curtains shut tight to keep in the warmth, the somber undeniable familiarity is alive inside the one-hundred-year-old, cherry wood home. Her walls split and crumbled over time, like me. It feels exactly right, the perfect 3:33 afternoon home. The rugs aged and frayed just so, remain the most comfortable spot to lose oneself and forget.

I lay my head on the carpet, ear nuzzled close to the ground, listening hard for my ancestors whispered truths. The dusk hour, I love the mysterious, raspy dusk hour when winding down begins and the light descends; and the bad spirits have yet to visit. The dusk hour is when I feel my closest to my dead. They are not gone from the earth, buried beneath the dirt, rotting maggots, and worms feeding on their bones. They are my living spirits, the blood, and guts, hard-working glue. These are my people. My ancestors, erect and honorable people, the pride and grace I come from. My off-kilter, filled to the brim loved ones.

· · ·

They steer the story, teaching me to stand on my own.

I am not angry. I am not angry at all. I'm not angry for the defective genes, the bad run of luck I have been, the unattractive parts of me. I am not even angry for the loss of the mind. That could not be helped; it is the necessary order of things. The walkabout was set in motion ages ago, lands ago, a million miles far and apart, way before I reached this blue people planet. To walk tall, wide-open, unafraid, wide-open, heavy fanatical head, the heart will never forget. That is the proud walk.

Tomorrow I can be angry. Tomorrow I will hurl blood-curdling screams, curses and fuck yous, fuck the whole goddamn lot of you for this curse upon my head. I did nothing to deserve this, except take in the first breath.

Not now though, not on this snow white, attractive 3:33 afternoon. Nope. Today, I am somber and moody reflective. I am unbelievably sad, moved by the melodic, golden variations. The dusk hour is melancholy and sorrow, a lovely, pensive time for what might've have been.

I would have been a good mother, I think. I would have raised a creative son. I would have taught him to build snow monsters and ginormous castles in the sun. We would've lounged on seashores and traveled to fancy, far away places. We would've lived a never-never land, happy, delightful existence. Coney Island would not have been reserved exclusively for Sundays.

I would have bought him his very own furry canine and taught him the meaning of firsts. I would've built him the perfect house to live in.

I would have shown him all the things I learned, the awful and the amazing, handing over keys to his very own kingdom.

I would have watched him become a proud, honorable man, from a healthy distance. I would've waited eagerly from a rusty, old red bench in summertime, for his return. I would've listened intently, while he recounted tales of a jovial life with a family of his own. I would have been delighted by these new beginnings, the possibilities on the road, a complete circle, and sacred walkabout.

Somewhere out there in the quiet, dusk afternoon, a newborn cries and is born without me. I never found him, but got lost in the story. My ancestors' still whisper their dreams, ancient rites and pagan rituals passed through dusty, dirty, faded, old carpet fiber afternoons. I listen intently through the wood and the planks, the dusk hour reserved exclusively for my ghosts.

Suddenly, I am less alone. The story keeps me alive and entertained, the mind is content to dwell in faraway places from the comfort of an antiquated, familiar home. Perhaps if I live a simple existence inside the magical dusk hour, I will find new life thriving on some parallel planet. I wonder if they hear the music, how haunting and lovely the sound.

A chill creeps over my bones. I need the red bench, my safe spot; this house has grown dark and alone.

HOUSE OF GLASS

There is something to be said about the sun. She wastes not one minute of precious time on worry. She hangs out, floating and spinning from a distance. She jams to reggae in the sky, giving us the juice to walk through the pitter-patter days. I am out west, where the evergreen mountains rise gloriously from the earth, the days start pretty, the sky tequila blue. The cool air and 70-degree sunny weather heal the broken parts. I am pieces put back together, yet still shaken to the core. I am weathered and seasoned beyond repair. I don't care if I live. I'm no longer vested in this earthly life, but the sun says otherwise.

There is no going back, back to the big city, back to the false living, back to the crazy feeling. There is no going back to the mad land and the Victorian walk, to the homeless version of me in search of a peaceful existence. I ignore the molecular mountains. I have a first class view of the landscape, the road before me.

I am the red bench, she lives in me, melded into a stronger version, her and I mixed up metal parts. I expect the fixings to be plenty, the tune-ups necessary. When in doubt, go back to the start. How do I walk this plentiful, sorrowful, angry, uneven path with dignity?

I miss my dead. This cannot be helped, it is human and I am the waking alien, emotional and messy. I look out my window from a luxury suite high in the heavens, sipping a latte, admiring the tabletop view. I laugh at myself, the struggle I have been. I cannot make amends with my luck, this gifted circumstance. It's funny and fleeting and stupid funny all over again.

Change is gnawing at my back; the woods swallow me whole. Bring me home back to the safest, coldest, darkest, gray spot I know. I don't mind the dark days, the bitter freeze, the seasonal shifts; I am comfortable in the backwoods. For today, I'll do nothing and soak up the sun. I'm going to store it in my cells, on my brain and use it as juice when I go back.

The right side is diversity alive and well, nature's beauty abundant, where jasmine and blue jays overflow, where the surf and beach are accessible in minutes. I could never live here, though it would be the perfect climate. The sky is wide open laughing, the oxygen clean. My modern, beach house of glass stands erect before me. It is at arm's reach, doors thrown open. I am the one that is stuck in the dark, sick and confused, perplexed and ugly.

I am not ready, I know. It's in the painful knots; the muscles screaming down my spine. The hate and anger yearn to explode. I work hard to live inside the pretty picture frame, yet beauty and happy escape me.

There is hard work to be done. It's closer than before, this thing called happy. Spring is inches away and I enjoy the seasons. The walk is circular, never flat, filled with shades of popular color. I am more beautiful exposed, without the plastic cover. I am multi-dimensional. The layers are plenty, bright, cobalt blue reds, dark angry grays and swampy forest greens.

I admit it. I love that. I love that piece of the madness. We build glass houses in our heads but rarely dwell in them. The sun is glorious and friendly and funny here on the right coast, but without the frigid cold waters, the snow and shadow seasons, the left loses her balance.

A thriller. Maybe I should write a thriller? Ah, hell no. Dirty, real life is way better than that. They are still there, the wicked thoughts. The visions of knives penetrating my skull, the bad days, the worms feasting on the brain, the demons, and angels duking it out, the sun and the crazy lady screaming at the sky fit nicely together. It's drama enough for a lifetime.

I don't know where the fuck I'm going, but the path has been cleared of snow. My perfect house of glass is the dreamy place as any, to start. The red bench is perched alongside this house. She follows me wherever I go. I forgot how much I loved jasmine and magnolia and the intoxicating smell of flowers, fruit trees, white linens, and nice, shiny things.

I am allowed to own one piece of pretty.

That is true courage, reclaiming the messy parts; the once important and beautiful lost art. The forgotten pieces discarded out of fear, madness and hasty decisions, all victims of harsh circumstance.

. . .

I'm merely liquid-solid; the walkabout and the dream propel me towards spring. I hope I can hold onto this contentment feeling and keep it safe, tucked away for the hard future. The inevitable, intolerable days when I can't remember my name. The days I walk my woods hunched and slow, the old lady more insane than before. The days where I waste away the minutes stuck in the memories, yearning to explode.

I hope I don't have to go back to the mad, mad existence, to a life fueled by imagination but I am willing to take the walk. The left and the right brain live on the fault line, falling straight down the middle. The sabbatical is the grace and tightrope balance, the luxury of choice.

The right coast is the perfect temperature for me, but I am choosing the left. It's where the red bench lives, and the sabbatical and the woods and the walkabout where family meaning and purpose hold me together

MELLOW YELLOW

Spring is here, and my resolve is firm. Three days of waking sunshine and the world feels better, less burdened by the weight of the formidable, unforgiving winter. Imagine my luck, I saw three robins on the path today. I'm sure I felt a semblance of a smile, followed by the rush of guilt. This newfound freedom entangled with the guilt of feeling the slightest bit better. The lunatic full of eccentricity, quirks, and paranoia on the brain lies dormant in far off corners. I love the woods, her buds in bloom. She and I have made it through another dark, frozen, frigid, treacherous winter.

Who can say for how long? I'll take it; these two seconds of clarity and happiness feel so much better.

I don't miss worldly possessions, the frivolous life. I went west one more time, testing the murky waters. How odd to live in Hollywood, the superficial land of make believe happy? Coming home, back to basics was the right move. How lucky am I? Home is the most fucked-up place on the planet, with all her weirdo characters moving about, full of strange creatures I don't fully understand. Yet, they get me and there are invaluable lessons to be learned from that. Home is where they love me stripped down. They love me loud, bright, black, fat, blasé, fanatical, ugly, in shades of manic red and living the dark angles, dreaming in black. They embrace all of me with a smile, knowing full well I am not perfect. They love me no less coloring my world pretty and coating the pages. They see me beautiful, more beautiful than I ever have.

They don't need urban makeup, stilettos, and shiny, twinkly things. They love the simplest version of me, the unique individual. They fight hard to keep me grounded in real time when I split apart and go missing. They encourage me when I am hurling false accusations, pacing and screaming at my least attractive. They guide me through the woods when I am lost. They don't bolt and take off when life is at its very worst.

I don't want to be different. I just want to be better than before. The red bench is good for that; she's the safest bet for the time being. The nomad and her backpack are quiet and settled, grateful for the stolen minutes. Happy to live her God-given red truths and fleeting days the best she can. I'm better, but not stupid. I've been granted a crazy time out, the healing necessity. I'm living the perfect be here now moment under no false pretense. My Parasol lady and I walk the regal life, the time stalled luxury.

The left coast suits me. The heavy, long winter has left a taste of spring on my tongue. I'm eager to plant, to create, to dream and to grow. I'm still touched by the mad angels, but better. I'm still paranoid, the residual glance over the shoulder omnipresent but better. I'm not able to venture out on my own but I am better, better than many seasons ago.

I can't stand the noise, the incessant shrieking annoying sounds, and aggravated voices. I can't stand the hate and indifference. Humans can be so cruel, so cold. Yet, I make peace with the nuisance and turn up the volume, shaking off the bad vibes. I turn up the music, masking all other noise. I close my eyes and will my mind to be quiet, to enjoy the solitude and fresh air. I'm better out here, in these backwoods. I'm the best I can be. No other place is better suited.

Spirit guides and ghosts live in these sacred Indian burial grounds, speaking to me. They hold my hand when I'm spiraling out of control. They show me an easier path on these sacred lands, a life in tune with nature. My story is no different than theirs; my story is no different than yours. My story is no better; I choose to find refuge on the page.

I'm counting on the words to unmask a sunnier tale. It's the same old story that's been written before; demons and angels, curses and families, genetic misprints, sorrow, disease, beaches, romance, red benches, puppy dogs, stars and alternate planets providing the backdrop for bittersweet, dark comedy. Still, I haven't told the story with its unique hues and waves of sea green, diamond drop white, bright stars and kooky cast of non-verbal characters. I have a clear new millennium, unobstructed view from this no place in particular, and forgotten corner of the world. Perhaps that makes the words new and honest again, richer than before.

It is, after all, just a life. No bigger, no better. I have breathed more shades, more pain, more joy, more crazy, more fear, more sadness than I thought possible to carry inside this one body. Death and daydreaming is my getaway car. I grasp tight to a red bench and wait, legs crossed and breathe in hope. Spring. I inhale deeply; the rich, evergreen sticky sweet smell permeates the air. I wait for the signs, small inklings of possibility. I look down towards the earth knowingly; season's change, haunting voices fade becoming chilling echoes of memory as new blossoms push their way through. God must be in control of something, as I pray to the sky and the sun and the music that lingers sweetly on the tongue. Underlying possibility and life's seasonal shifts are the gifts. We are nature's finest and saddest creation, faceless shadows fading over time in all her mysterious torture and glory. Painting a circular picture, I walkabout. Gray seasons turn black to white, and mellow yellow sunflower fields grow the perfect summer backdrop.

I don't know how my story will end. I can't see it, but I can feel the sun inside the melody. I soak up the warmth on my face, in my bones and on my skin breathing in the sultry colors. Summer hangs out around the corner; my mystic glass beach house of windows is inches out of reach. Sadie love lives in my dreams and waits patiently for the perfect cosmic moment when our stars align, bringing her and me together.

My birthday falls in spring; I'm lucky I'm told. I have made it through another harsh, mind-altering and unforgiving winter, healthier than before.

My retreat heals the broken parts, giving the words heartfelt meaning. That is all I can hope, that seasons to continue to come and go, and the walk gracefully remains. Others have come and gone, and many will come after. I will be less than an afterthought, a speckle of dust floating on a cloud of air. I don't mind, there is freedom in flying weightless; I'll find my mother and father dwelling there. And the mystery goes on without us much like before.

I walk today with more resolve, focus, care, thought, good nature, and strength than five minutes ago. This simple act of courage keeps me on track.

CARNY DAYS

There are days meant to create, and others to stand still. There are days when the sun hides from the earth, hoarding precious vitamins and leaving only death-gripping depression. Lately, I have not been my best self. I have not been well. I've been preoccupied, busy fighting the tilt a whirl in my head.

The dizzying vortex, spinning nausea, the endless terror, and the relentless, out of control spiraling drains me. I am exhausted. I have lost all avenues of reason. I wait for the drugs to kick in, for the dosage to readjust, the guessing game between modern medicine man and me. I long for the battle to be over, to exist inside the walls of sanity.

These are the days when the walk seems impossibly long, wet and mundane. These are the days I lose control, tears wet my face and snot flow from my nose, the mania and anxiety all-consuming. The numbness creeps in like a bad habit, the persistent ill state of being.

I will not give in to this life sentence of disease. I will make light of the impossible heavy. I will sob inconsolably, waking at night soaked through the sheets, tossing in my sleep from terror and folly. I pray on my knees. I bargain with the devil offering bits and pieces of my brain. For one ignorant spilt second, I imagine the madness is done with me. But no, I am not that lucky. She digs her nails deeper into my resolve, ripping normalcy apart.

I do not walk to my woods. I run. It's sodden, damp and dreary. Nothing seems inviting or pretty. I don't care. I cuss, I curse, I scream, I pace, holding the sides of my head, waiting for the explosion. I will not go down that easy. I hang on to science, to theory, to the words of my mother that change is ever present and insanity is temporary. Depression is the cruel jester, relentless and unforgiving. Faith, ignorance and stubborn thinking have carried me to this halfway mark of uncertainty. I want to feel the sun; I want to feel happy. I want to believe sanity is possible, that the ancient rituals and nurturing woods might fix me. Magically mend the broken parts.

Oh dear, where is my Parasol lady? Has she forgotten our time together? Is she off in some other dimension sauntering amongst kings and queens? Does the light shine on her illuminating her world? Are kindness, splendor and loud love there, guiding her beyond the ether? Are her days bright and lighthearted? Are her needs met with a certain kind of ease?

She was I once upon a time, living without a care, a selfish kind of existence. I was the gypsy flitting across the globe, never stopping for a second. I moved in haste, not giving a moment's pause. I will her to be here, my elegant, polka dot parasol lady so I might move freely and follow a few paces behind her elegant footing.

I close my eyes and breathe deep, choking on air and contempt. I do it again with more fervor. Jesus endured much worse. I can do this. If I can manage one full breath, perhaps she will come. I wait a long, long time, an empty while. She never appears. I find myself soaking wet in bed with night terrors instead. Stuck in some foreign land, lost in a hailstorm, while living out the nightmare.

I'm cold, shivering and forgotten. I lie buried in rough sand, my skin bleeding and burning. I try to regain my bearings. That's when I see it. Shocked and disgusted, I can't believe what's directly in front of me. The mind wreckage, another pile of heaped up delusion.

My perfect beach house is in shambles, crumbling to the ground. The windows on my wall of glass modern home are rotted, broken and in ruins from the elements and the storm. The house sits abandoned, sad and unwanted. The grass has grown wild, magnolia bushes left to die, brittle and untended. The ominous, black ocean is tumultuous, the waves wild and the water freezing. The sea is menacing angry and the sand is gritty and blood scratching.

My red bench has been chipped apart, ripped from her post and eaten alive by rust. I am devastated, crushed by the vision. I never make it back to tend to the lovely gardens. How unbelievably sad, the misty shades of gray with no sun. I lost my way, brainwaves got crisscrossed and neurological wires misfired leaving me lost. Oh, how I loved the dream. I cringe at the horrible sight I'm seeing. I want to go home and out of this tailwind headspace, back to all the pretty places I've seen.

I'm living the carny life, riding a tilt a whirl with no emergency stop button. Mindful and stubborn, I dig deeper for a way out. I barter with God who has been loosely absent, promising away parts of my soul to the devil. I am the downward spiral trapped in a foreign world, way harder and way longer than usual.

I awake suddenly out of the misty haze, unfocused mind to a less menacing sky. It's as if the cloud cover has magically lifted and drifted far out to sea, the oceans calm and clear. I am in familiar surroundings. I look down and catch a glimpse of the pristine red metal and breath in a choked sigh of relief. My bench stands shiny and solid, she has not moved out of sight. I am back after a long, lengthy and precarious out of my mind absence.

I sit all alone, adrift between too many worlds and one head. I am content with the present, the brisk air that is spring. I am freed from the unpleasant memory and the mind forgets, losing interest in carny dreams and endless meager matter at four percent.

BYE-BYE BIRDY

I fear I cannot keep this up, this charade of a life. I fear I am too tired, too weary to dance the frenetic mind dance. I can't see the horizon from this twirling velocity, the neat and pretty outcome. The red robin lands on my doorstep, after the long winter's freeze and the bitter, drawn-out months. She is beautiful, in all her robust color, regal red and maternal glory. I am bound to shoo her off, the nuisance.

She returns countless times in spite of failed attempts at safe landing, eager to build her nest only to find the pathway blocked. This is not my doing. I am not in charge of this house. In these days, it feels as if I am powerless and the head of nothing. Summoning stubbornness I resist, retaining the smallest sliver of pride.

There is no harmony between nature and tidy living. I could care less. I don't give a fuck over mindless thinking. Let the birds and animals take over, wrap this house in a cocoon so that I might be strangled alive, trapped securely hiding in place. This is not a life worth living. I did not come here to be a mere spectator, unable to participate.

I have lost too much battling rapid cycling. I have lost friends, forgone ease, independence, left behind outdated ways, given up the desire to venture out, discover new lands, new ideas, opportunities, and fresh ways of thinking. I am paralyzed, stuck in the same spot, terrorized by the thought of venturing out. Anxiety pulsates inside my chest choking and closing my throat.

The red bench has grown tired of my shallow mad existence, the narcissistic way of thinking. To go mad is to become the ultimate narcissist, the incessant over-thinker spiraling hard and fast, deep into self- obsession. The rain does not help, nor does the dreary, dark town I live in. I've been here before, a million times adrift in and out of reality, floating along this odd, blue people planet.

Most days I adapt, fake a forced smile to coexist, allergic to my mind as it refuses the numbing drugs and ups the voltage. I must conform and pretend, pretend that I am present and willing. None of that is true. I'm the adult, buried in responsibility and drowning on delusion. I've squashed all hope for the red robin's nest. I murdered them, compliant to rules from someone else's playbook. What if I can't accept that I am indeed going to die from insanity, even if cancer kills me first?

Snow falls on the grass on this almost May day and the trees are already in pink petal bloom. What the fuck is happening? Global warming has her own plans shaking things up on this insignificant, tiniest piece of the puzzle planet earth. I am happy with the ugly, backward mess. Perhaps my robin has a shot at building her nest somewhere else. I won't walk today, but will curl up in silence and self-protection, closing my eyes instead; drifting off and dreaming about the circular walk will suffice.

In my dreams, I envision an altogether different version of myself; a younger, happier, slender, soft-edged person with a more vibrant future mapped out. She still dreams in Kodachrome where puppies, beach homes and neat, parasol living abounds. Where dazzling, bright white planets are stars full of possibility. In her dreams, sparkling yellow sunbeams glisten from her eyes. She has yet to be poisoned, injected and force-fed pills, psychosis, and brutal realities.

This girl has a shot. A real, do over shot at happy. As long as the imagination has not been stolen, she has the dream to hold onto.

I endure the brutal, harsh days until something bigger than fear; self-loathing and death can take hold. I live the limitations with a certain air of grace, donning the best quiet mask I can. As long as there is hope, that God will not abandon me in these uncertain times I continue, resolute. I swallow the uneven, shallow breath, however difficult. I have the whole day to work on it, finding air that is easier and smoothed out.

The robin forgives me my simple, humane existence. She knows I am following the orders of the house. I am a guest in this one-hundred-year-old house that carries her own shady past, secrets, and lies, the ghost-filled history. I am simply at the mercy of time. I will endure with whatever shred of dignity I can muster.

To never forget the words. The page carries me when I cannot stand, crouched in the fetal position on the bathroom floor. The page creates big dreams when I see nothing through misty eyes. The page promises hope when I have exhausted all roads and left dreaming behind. The page holds my hand and guides me towards words that are a wee bit lighter. The snow has lost interest in this corner of the continent and gone off to find glaciers and ice caverns, more appropriate temperatures to visit.

The earth is damp and sloppy. It is the perfect, moist soil rich for spring planting. I chose perennials in fantastic rainbow colors, planting them with love and reassurance. I cure these seedlings with care and attention and with the humanistic, egotistical hope they will return for many years after I am gone. There is sad, sweet unbearable love in the choices made over the course of a lifetime. My choice to continue planting is highly personal, in spite of all the madness and uncertainty that lies ahead.

I love the sweet-smelling purples, the sultry inviting reds, and the tropical fuchsia buds emerging from the earth. I cultivate my garden with a deep affection for spring and the seasons that follow. In my magical garden, I am not too sick to plant, to feel young and giddy with shock and awe each time spring bores hope in glorious color. It reminds me of all that has come before, the gorgeous, carefree, happy, healthier time, and easier existence. All the odd, kooky characters that make up my life, the very real, and not imagined ones. The ones I have loved far too much, way beyond any possible earthly explanation. Those responsible for cultivating all the sappy, sweet, fun flowering pieces of my heart, curing them with care and healing devotion.

The page finds my robin her perfect nesting grounds, granting sunshine; cloudless days and warmth, where bird nests round eggs grow safe and healthy. She is pleased; I am pleased as I watch. My face pressed up against the cool glass from a chair near the window, dreaming of the world I once lived in.

. . .

The May snow magically disappears, melting away worry inside the damp, greedy earth. I leave anxiety on the page and get on with the day venturing out, planting and tending my garden's rebirth. Thunder roars and rain trickles down never touching the soil. The seasons however unpredictable are funny like that. The sun shines from behind thick cloud cover, mixing up the day with mercurial moods and vortex swirls of emotion. I laugh at the impermanence and three-second-mishmash storm from the heavens, the reminder of how fickle and fleeting life is. We are nothing more than ordinary beings, meager matter at a small percent.

Another tempest looms overhead, I don't fret about the daunting black cloud cover. I welcome the cool, fresh breeze instead.

COTTON-PUFF CLOUDS AND CRYSTAL CLEAR SKY

The occasional cotton-puff cloud floats by as I lay in the grass contemplating the sideways life. The afternoon's heat and scorching sun are unbearable. Lazy fresh Maydays have disappeared turning June into a sticky, prickly high heat.

My alternate life, where Sadie love lives content in our pristine, cozy white, open-air beach home is the dream of choice. I am the unsick; free to write novellas and gut-wrenching stories filled with meaning for the scared and lost souls. I dress in carefree, out of date comfortable clothes. The kitchen is pristine, silver and modern, filled with contemporary appliances. The fridge is stocked with a multitude of colorful fruit and rich, leafy vegetables for the heart, healthy mind.

I don't cook. I don't have to. Meals are prepared on a whim. It's the uncomplicated life where I'm serene, and the ocean's waves lullaby me to sleep. It's sacred space where Sadie love is always at my feet. It's the capable life, one I can manage quite well on my own. Our walk always happens in the afternoon, when the day has cooled and the sun prepares to set. We walk for miles and miles no ticking clock or timetable demands. We walk the empty beach for miles and miles alone, exclusively ours. We don't even mind the occasional tourist. Sadie bounces up to say hello and we get on with it, familiar with the seashell path and the happy structure of routine in the afternoon. I love it on this isolated beach, in this sanctuary home.

I am my best self, allowed a moment of respite to forget the exhaustion and the fight of a battle that cannot be won. The disease has stolen fragments of my fractured mind and played dirty, rotten tricks on me, making it impossible to separate reality from fantasy. I find myself alone; there is no modern wall of glass beach home. I never see anyone from the blue people planet with me inside the dream. I only see numbing solitude, and respite, a world I desperately hold onto to fill in the caverns of a shattered brain.

My sideways life has her faults, I suppose. There is an only one-sided conversation, and the days are shades of the same color. The bench appears blue and depressed, that will never do. In my heart, soul, and mind I know my bench is saucy, fire engine red. Burning with life's passions, curiosity, drama, suspense, mystery, and sorrow. Joy, hope, and wonder live there too. It's the best safe spot I visit when anxiety, madness, and death have taken hold. It is mad, brilliant escapism, no matter the pain and sorrow I must endure. We walk together; me and the kooky characters that cross my path. Some are alive in real time, while others exist in alternate universes and sideways worlds, figments of an overactive imagination. I have come to believe life is better when shared with imperfect souls, even when the mind doesn't want company and plays rapid cycling trickery.

I miss my spirit guides, the ancestors who came before. I can't hear their voices sweetly nudging me towards the right path. My head is mangled by the sheer volume and terror of too many thoughts turning inside out, lacking the necessary oxygen for calm. When I was younger and unburdened by the weight of insanity, I felt them close. I welcomed the spirit presence. I so hope they are off free flying and hanging out without regret or worry until I am in their company again.

I am alone, so awfully lonely. But oddly, I am not. I am rarely alone except when off dreaming of some other planet, walking amongst queens and puppy dog tails. My beach house is the secret haven I share to cope and the red bench is the sacred, safety zone. It's the balancing out place where bad thoughts and good vibes return to neutral. It's a just world, where most babies are born happy and healthy. Where the aged die without grace and dignity, surrounded by their beloved if they're lucky.

In death, the slate is wiped clean and the words move any way they see fit. The sabbatical has no preset time stamp, nor does the journey. For the moment, I must endure more pain than one should have to carry. Beyond the ether, I cannot go.

GARDEN OF ZEN

I am exactly where I wanted. I have mapped out a small piece of destiny, perfectly and cautiously orchestrated over the long, headstrong winter months. I've thrown away flashy, opting for serenity. The woods and walk are my most natural state of being. I'm filled with the knowledge and terror there is no perfect existence, it's millisecond moments of bliss and fleeting, futile, horseshit. The red bench is overcrowded with strangers. How odd, blue people out for a summertime stroll. I hate them, these intruders laughing, playing, enjoying the mild temperatures, invading my spot and peace of mind. I hate them for being sane; I despise me for being sick. I wish for winter and the polar vortex, so they might dissolve into liquid air and I am cocooned again in silence.

I do not fair well amongst humans. I do better with ghosts and spirits, parasol ladies, homeless kings and queens dancing around my head. I have not found solace amid the living. Try as I may to quell the summer lightning flashes and rolling thunderstorm thrashing about my brain, I don't succeed. Shush, for the love of Christ. Please keep down the goddamn noise, so I might find my way back to peace and quiet.

Is this my fate, perpetual dissatisfaction? I try to be the bigger person; building my garden of Zen but find I am less capable than the rest. I dig deep searching for anything in common, living in a myopic world. Contradiction, frenzy, greed, rage, envy, and hate are the themes of a new millennium. I want no part of the rat race, the ridiculous lust for things out of reach. I'll take a healthy mind over matter, and strong body in perfect sync. June's budding flowers bring fresh blood cruising through my veins delivering much-needed brain oxygen. The head nurtures the body harvesting robust seedlings and strong roots, making rainbow colors look lovely and pineapple gardens taste sweet.

What difference do the mad genes make when everyone is off running in circles? The velocity of my thoughts makes up for the snail pace of the body, and aching limbs. I pray one might balance out the other. The monotony of the same old, boring tedious routine gives structure to the wandering head. The walkabout has come to a screeching halt; words escape me, uncertain of this new pace. Diamonds dance and stars dazzle the sky at night, and wet grass tickles my feet as I gaze up dreaming of an entirely different life. The moon illuminates my course, as I spin around and around in circles growing dizzy. Humming in the dark, the five-year-old undamaged by disease relies solely on instinct and bliss. I reach down grazing the dew and green blades of grass, blowing a wet kiss towards infinity and my dead, free from this place. I carry on. I must. I must walk in circles wandering while praying for clarity and straight thinking.

I shrug my shoulders, recalling the first step towards happy. Discovering new lands, beaches, crystals, moonbeams, and shiny, purposeful things. I retrace those first steps. There was a time I was whole, there was a time I was happy, beautiful and bold. There was a time when choking breath and red bench security were unnecessary. I was sane and fit perfectly inside the picture frame.

Oh, how I hate society's boxes and codes and rules of conduct. Fuck off conformity. Mad folly allows for unrestricted morality, collecting starfish and seashells on a whim, turning black and white words into shiny, twinkly paper messages illuminating the night. I am lucky like that. I am blessed with the unique, thought-provoking creative process. God has not stripped away all the magic or the mystery. I become less and less attached to the cells and molecules in the body; I am less concerned with the blue people and her planet opting for the artist's way instead.

I walk the woods deep in thought, dreaming up made up worlds. In my head, the battle is deeply personal and scores are settled, toxic brain matter chewed up and spit out. God is an afterthought, where personal pain is not so horribly hard to manage; and mortality takes a back page in the story. Fantastical life always has room to flower and grow.

The numbness travels up and down my veins, forcing me back to reality. My head swirls a million miles a minute, it's not enough to make me give up. So fuck you paranoia, and fuck off demons. I have no patience for idle mediocrity. I carry suicide tucked away in my back pocket for a later date. I type away, weaving the tale and a place that's kind enough to stay, refusing the cliché and certain tragic death. The pain is real, ever present, physical, critical and draining away my life, and my willpower. Still, I won't give in without a fight motherfucker. If I live in the land of type, easy summer days become the reality leading the way to joyful, lazy days and long life.

. . .

My manic depressive head is another space and time dimension, the new normal, an alternate universe I can't recover from or makeup. I am liquid-solid I recall, floating freestyle above the crazy; it's the easiest train of circular thought. My garden is plenty and full of the exotic; inviting purples, reds, yellows, fuchsias and periwinkles color the day, fireflies and sweet magnolia perfume the night.

And so I go on, planting a Zen life.

LAVENDER FIELDS OF HEAVY

My burning, swollen numb, unbearably aching feet won't let me escape. I can't run, barely able to walk and stand on my own. The unruly mind and scorching, oppressive summer heat burn and blisters the soles on this stifling hot, one hundred degrees day. If only I could enjoy the pretty, lavender hazed filled days I'd be free. Free from the stereotypes of insanity and how I think it should be.

I ignore them, the small-minded blue people's wants and futile desires, living far from dark society. I am solely and purposefully on sabbatical, growing restless of the seasonal, circular routine. The conundrum and dis-ease brew heat storms in the brain, playing summer tricks. Lithium does not appreciate the unforgiving humidity, swelling the extremities.

The homeless lady prefers cooler temperatures; her cart and meager belongings melt and rot in the heat. She cannot avoid her rancid smell, swearing, pacing, cursing, and flailing recklessly in heated discussion with the air. The far off, far away aqua blue ceiling offers no relief. There is no luxury here if only she could escape to a beach. There is room enough for her in the beautiful land of make believe, the wall of glass home by the sea. I offer her a spot all her own, the vast ocean to cleanse and roam free. She won't join me in heaven, stuck in some horrible hell bound to devils and demons, the dark voices living in her head. Surely I will drown, weighted down by dilemma if I can't convince her to join me.

Sadie lovely comes close, sensing the sadness upon me; she places her paw on my lap while nuzzling her sweet face, grateful and content I am alive and with her. Melancholy swallows me whole. I am blessed there is one creature that accepts and understands my state of mind.

I stand up, shaking off the blues and head out. I am not selfish; Sadie must walk. We spend countless hours outdoors, getting lost in nature, mesmerized by the beach and the sea. I am happy she takes me away from the dark places and ugly thoughts. We stop at the red bench to rest before entering our welcoming home. Her water bowl waits under the chair, palms shading us from the sun. She and I sit for a long, long while enjoying our shelter and the calm.

I frolic in the ocean, diving deep beneath the waves basking in the beautiful silence and mysterious colors of the sea, my mind capable of the journey. In an instant, the body becomes weightless and sea salt drains the sharp, relentless pain from my feet. I am lighter than ever before. The body and muscle memory cool down to manageable, no longer suffering the long, drawn-out summer heat.

I must record this happy feeling, store it deep in the recesses of the mind. It's the precious, fleeting memory of contentment, clarity that comes and goes in an instant. Shooting magic imagery that burns out before you can grab hold. I wonder if my homeless lady has ever felt that kind of pure, blissful minute. I doubt that she has found any relief from the shallow, hollow, hard, mad outcast existence.

It's the empty fairground illusion and déjà vu feeling, long after the carnival has packed up and gone. The grounds left eerily deserted. Shaman winds twist and turn, conjuring hearty summer rains, washing clean humanity's imprint. Its goosebumps of delight on the skin, a lucky penny and forgotten dream, dirty fishbowls of rainbow colored water, antiquated jovial carnal fun. It's the frivolous frail, the innocence of a child, carefree and full of wonder. Holding tight to the earliest happy memory, she recalls her big and strong daddy's, all-encompassing love. He makes sense in her world and loves a good carnival, the sticky, sweet treats and fried dough smells, flashing strobe light carny rides, squeals, and shrieks of laughter. She touches her wrist in angst, searching for the lost cheap neon bracelet lighting the night and illuminating her way home.

I do hope my homeless lady has experienced one clear minute when the stars aligned and left her in peace. Far from ego, worry, pain, disease, death, adulthood, far from gravity and the irrational pull towards earth. I want for her the same as I want for me, a light-hearted, simple life where universal woods and the walk is enough. Where a red bench provides the necessary safety cushion and earth's dance is alive with naked abandon and primal passion. Where boxed in rules need not apply. Where dirty is sexy clean, and lavender fields bloom all season. Where crazy is sanity making perfect sense and the mirror is unbroken, where stars shine brightest during the day and Borealis hues light the sky at night. I dance on the ceiling in honor of her and me, and the child who has been forgotten. The smell of cotton candy washed away with the acrid reality of madness.

Music and the pitter-patter of the typewriter keys make for a beautiful haunting, meteoric symphony. Sweet sorrow memory is the waltz; classic, timeless art in perfect step with the carnival, the characters and the empty, forlorn, abandoned, long ago forgotten desert.

I bend down as I walk, and find a chewed up plastic, brittle neon bracelet buried under the rocks in the dirt. Much like an archeologist discovering precious artifacts, I smile with the heartwarming truth. I am reminded of a prettier place and happy days. A tear runs down my cheek replenishing the dry, cracked, discarded red earth. I know it to be true on my skin in an instant; I have indeed been content. Despite living and breathing amongst beggars, liars and shopping cart freaks, the dreamer still believes in beaches, parasol queens and lapping puppy dog kisses has been enough.

It is far from the perfect shadow box life, but time moves along however unsteady, in and out of sync. The sideways life, the salt-shaker reality, and the dream make the trivial, mundane, horrible, hard, heavy days bearable. Almost. I drop one seed from my pocket into the earth and pray, letting my tears give faith root. Perhaps in some alternate universe far and away from here, an all-together different molecular life takes shape, where lavender fields grow plenty taking over deserted, abandoned lots.

Liquid-solid becomes modified by temperature; the homeless lady transforms into a queen with stunning gilded, orchid angel wings, taking on a new, twinkling charmed, more luxurious life.

I did not come here to wait. I did not come here to be stuck, in some bubble of ill regret. I came here to dance in between the lines and live dimensionless, weightless and free, dividing equal time in the woods and by the beach. Making peace with the mind's duality rooted deep in reality and reckless abandon.

Dreaming is free; it costs nothing but a bit of youth and pieces of memory, colorful, careless wonders of the mind and fragmented imagination.

New Mexico sounds like the perfect place to me. Surrounded by the heat and the vast landscape desert, shooting stars and hazy, pink ceiling. Parasol queens and kings thrive out West, basking under a blue moon sky. The carny stops a while taking time to rest and replenish, relishing the ancient burial grounds, cacti, and wide-open spaces.

CRINOLINE AND LACE

Oh no, this cannot be happening. My parasol queen is dead. She died alone, buried in the woods beneath the trees and decaying apples. Her heavy corsets, bustle, and crinoline melted in the August heat. We didn't get the chance for a final walk, a proper goodbye. I will dig her a fitting grave, lovingly drape her in sateen and jewels fit for a queen, placing her gently on her back gazing towards the sky's ceiling for eternity. She is liquid nothing now, mere particles in heaven, and a figment of my overzealous imagination. I will miss her, nonetheless.

She was my one true friend over the mad seasons, alternate planets and various times zones. We talked about many things, the fun stuff and philosophy too. Sometimes we remained silent and just walked, wasting away the day. She taught me to be a lady, showed me an easier way to be brave and stand erect, shrugging off shame and self-hatred. She was a small piece of me, the stealth-minded Victorian queen, and I was her lady in waiting.

· · ·

She left me her whimsical, hot pink polka dot parasol to shade the New Millennium unforgiving sun, in times of extreme heat. She promised we would meet again, under an altogether different moon, so that we might relive leisurely days well spent. I loved her, madly. I am sad, yet not sorrow. She gave me the greatest gift, the chance to just be, at peace in our woods. Over the long, hard winter months, fall, spring, and summer I learned many things.

I knew our time together would end. I had an inkling I would lose the vision but hoped I would not.

A chance encounter can change the course of everything; depressed months that drag on, and the manic free fall of fast-paced thinking proved a parasol queen and mere mortal can, in fact, get along. Growing true friendship that outlasts the course of ordinary blue people's folly, and the charlatan's lifetime.

I knew I would lose her when the mind parts began to disappear, and reality returned. Maybe it's the sun on my face, the heat on my skin. Perhaps it's God's way of balancing out the madness, releasing her and giving me back a small piece of sanity. I'm not sure I want it; the characters in my head have been steadfast and true. In it for the long haul, she was more real to me than the mortals rendered angry, powerless, and out of touch. Sadie's love, the beach house, and my homeless visitors take her place. They are the bizarre, off-putting characters wise enough to fill the empty space. People can be so cruel and oblivious, unable to grasp the nature of an invisible, unruly mind. It makes the crushing solitude unable to bear, wishing I were dead.

I run to the red bench, the safest place I know. I sit quietly and reflect. Shedding tears for lost love and bits of my broken heart. Somber and grateful, I reflect on all that has gone, the heavy price she and I paid. The insight and fantasy gained walking side-by-side, donning lace and sateen. I don't dare hope insanity is finished with me; I am not that naïve. I say a prayer for my queen's departure and loss of imagination instead.

I count the butterflies that flitter over the grass, in sublime color, orange, yellow, powder blue and brazen white. The doe and her babies graze upstream. Chipmunks scurry along the path, and so it is. Life carries on. I am alive inside the shell of a being, the sun tells me so. I feel it on my face, the skin is warm under the handsome, August eggshell sky. It is not a scorching day, but a pleasant heat. I am alive and well on this day even with a sullen, heavy heart. My queen lives inside me, I know exactly which parts I will summon if need be. I hope she returns from another dimension, some far away mystical place in the recesses of my mind.

The red bench is embedded in the ground, I am happy to wander the woods. Perhaps later, I will head out to the beach and take a long, long swim with Sadie love filling her in on my day. There is much writing to be done, and time is running thin. My antique, wooden desk waits inside the stark, modern house. The black and white pitter-patter of the keys grows anxious to finish the story.

I can feel it in my bones; the night air confirms it. Summer is coming to a close, the story and twelve-month sabbatical are nearly finished. The brainwaves are calm and the sea air is moist. My skin is thankful for the blues of the ocean. I grab a sarong, wrapping the white thread over my shoulders preparing myself for a much needed, well-deserved nap.

· · ·

The dusk sky is my favorite, pink and orange haze hues whisper her name so I don't forget. My parasol queen lies curled up beside me in memory. Revisiting the mysterious duality of the high and low tide, mesmerized by the undercurrents and the lull of the ocean, I fall fast asleep.

SERRATED EDGE

The drugs mask the murderer within, the rage, the savage beast. I could kill with the slip of the tongue. Snap a neck for the simplest wrongdoing. There is too much rotten angst living inside me. The angry, irritable two-year-old, spoiled rotten self is frustrated and misunderstood. Banging her head against the wall, she is unable to express the right emotion, the injustice she endures.

The ignorant, ego-driven society fuels my disgust. Twist a knife in obesity's gut; the protruding, excess redneck belly of gluttony makes me sick. Do not speak. I won't listen. I don't care about you consumed with fantasy and the self-obsessed life. I don't care if the kitchen is clean, the clothes washed, the house neat. What good is paper box living, when parasol queens are left to evaporate in the dirt?

I exist in a world created for one, where fairy tales make for easier living. Ripped apart by the small, manic, hollow, and worthless existence the dark thoughts strangle me whole. Wrapped up and tangled together, muddled in the writing. I feel nothing. I am black nothing, numb thinking, the bottomless tar pit devours me whole.

The shopping cart queen is crazy disgusting, an embarrassment amongst the living. I am millimeters away from her existence, the stench a rude awakening. The leech mind sucks up the good, faster than I can rework clear thinking. It's only August, the darkness usually waits for winter to descend.

Maybe the red bench can't me save me, despite her noblest effort.

I despise people, the hovering and ignorance. Stupid, simpletons how do they just get on with it, when I die a bit more each minute? They can't see the ruptured fragments, the shaky uncomfortable me, the blood curdling screams at night in my pillow. They don't understand the uncertainty, the unforgiving days I must navigate. I spare them the dark thoughts in my head; the slight twitch of an eye conceals the insanity.

I hide the dirty, ugly business, and walk. I do not walk but run the mind. I run through my thoughts. I do not walk; walking is the luxury for the enlightened. I race to the red bench and repeat my mantra. Begging for forgiveness for the cruel thoughts, asking for the quickest way back. Show me the conclusion, I dare say. I waste not another word, not one more page, one more type, no more day-dreaming cocooned in fantasy.

If I held the key to the secrets that could unlock life's mystery, meaning, and purpose, and the foresight to see beyond my meager existence, would I listen? Maybe one swift cut of the blade is all that's needed, a quick slice of the sharp, serrated edge against the base of the throat. A precise, neat motion severs the neck bone, obliterating life, as I knew it. Maybe I could coax the shopping cart queen to do it? I could bribe her with pills and fancy things, filling her cart with the latest fads. Who am I kidding? I am the coward, while she is honest living. I am the indecisive, the barely alive undead left out in the rain.

The walkabout is the one true thing. It pulls me out of the black hole, giving me time to regroup. Red bench security, the comforting safety zone squashes away the evil in my head. Just yesterday my parasol queen and I revisited her death, and I was filled with the smallest glimpse of hope, and tiniest sliver sense of purpose. How fast one forgets. What a farce, this human life. I am nothing, shallow liquid nothingness, molecules and cells at the lowest, miserly percent.

Crazy is the main character driving the tale, she steals all the empty space in my head. Taking over and taking control, she drives the story. I am merely the physical nuisance filling space, locked inside the diabolical head.

Mad folly is all consuming. It invades more and more of the healthy, brain parts. Swallowing the blue person whole, devouring bliss for the fun of it. Each day she claims more and more clarity, stealing away memory and brain matter. I won't do it.

I won't disintegrate into nothingness without a fight and raw guts determination.

However tired I am of this ping-pong volley, however physically and emotionally spent. I won't give her the satisfaction, leaving me naked and exposed, discarded like useless waste material. The insect, the squashed afterthought left to die in the dirt. No, I won't quit. When the demons and voices tell me to end it I close the blinds, turn down the volume and go radio silent. I wait out the storms and the squalls, summoning happy memory and the stillness of easy minutes.

Fuck off bitch, go away and leave me this life to live it, anyway I see fit. I am as stubborn and hardcore as the evil that is you. One way or another I shall force my way back, where you no longer have a say in it. For now, I sit rocking back and forth, cradling my head in my hands, confused, tortured, and self-deflated.

Is this me? Have I been reduced to live in worlds I know not?

I must flee, hide in the dusty, dirty rafters overhead. The serrated edge glistening in my hand, beckons. I see the distraught image through the shiny, mirror surface of the blade, and wipe away tears filled with an ocean of regret.

I must not forget, never ever forgo this one shot at an honest life. A well-played beginning, hold on tight middle, and the serene, graceful, beloved end. I have been given this jewel of a life for a reason. Loosening my grip on the serrated edge I grab tight to the rafters overhead.

Sleep being a key element, I close my eyes and nod off in a purple mist, hazy fog. I watch as sawdust slowly dances through the air, coloring the space with splintered diamonds and specks of sparkling wood. Ancient, sacred jewels of wisdom past down from ghosts of regret, time, and circumstance.

BURSTS OF RED OCEAN

I saw bursts of red; out of place amiss the evergreen. At first, I thought, how lovely a cardinal lives in the brush. Ah, but alas it was not. It was just leaves, fire engine red in the middle of summer? It's not the middle anymore; it's nearer the end. We are mid-month August, and September's around the corner. A few more minutes and she'll be here in all her seasonal, splendid glory.

I don't mind. I love September, the month. Perhaps, it is my favorite. The air is just cool enough, the days the perfect length, and night air brisk and honeyed. Much has changed over the course of an almost complete year. I have let go of many things but am still required to move forward. The tortured mind dwells inches below the surface. I work hard to let it be, leave her alone.

The spirits and voices are much quieter now; I summon them less.

I walk the remainder alone.

. . .

I walk, and I wait. I wait for something bigger. I sit on the bench and reflect. I remind myself of the ebb and flow from deep inside the sanctuary of a forest. My shopping cart lady is out, enjoying the mild breeze. She is clean today, her hair tidy, and clothes neat. She keeps her hands in a fist, dangling loosely at her side. She is oddly calm, the bizarre rant's gone silent.

I look closer at her face gasping; she resembles me exactly. How odd. She is less humane, her dance and song primal, naked and exposed. She doesn't care if she stinks to the high heavens, curses, and spits in front of your children. She is free, free, free to release the devil living in her head. She doesn't worry about the superficial and doesn't need the high drama. She is humanity at its purest, not always pleasant to look at and shockingly true to the senses. She is raw energy, free-flowing liquid at the highest percent. She is more me, more honest and unapologetic than most. She is God's imperfectly perfect creature, isn't she?

She wears no mask and doesn't hide her sorrow, pain, and bad luck of a life. She is reckless and free. She doesn't let hate rule her choices, she knows no better. She is me off the meds, never given a chance. Her voice has been stifled, wracked by disease. She has been told to keep quiet or act appropriately. She does not listen. The flies and the noise buzzing inside her brain make it hard to focus. Shhh, turn down the volume I say, while she screams TURN IT UP! She knows no shame, regret, social stigma or dis-ease. The blue people put labels on her cart to avoid her, placing obstacles along her way.

She does not try to reclaim lost sanity, mend broken relationships, or pick up the shattered pieces of a life, again and again. She does not offer an apology or worry over false pretenses. She does not hide, preoccupied with busyness, or waiting on the death box. She rides out the squalls in the streets reckless and unapologetic. She rarely waits for low tide before jumping headfirst, into the uncharted. I envy her I do; her freedom is a thing I envy and forget.

Someday our roles will reverse. And I will be her, carefree and unwilling to conform to the neat, tidy, cement plaster box. I say fuck you medicine, fuck you world, fuck you stereotypes bring on the mad folly. She and I will be allies, kooky characters, and partners in crime. Free from the hard, heavy midway points, free from the thousand-plus days spent fighting. Free from the desire of something more, free from the out of reach I am not. Free from the blue people and the alien planet. I will be dust, lightning bugs, margaritas, and blue moon, starry evenings. Purple snow cones readily available; magically turn yellow and blue on a whim, sour and sweet to the taste. I will delirious and delicious, all at once.

I close my eyes and will it. Sanity. I remind myself, the sabbatical is not finished. The battery operated clock on the wall tells me so, ticks the tock. I must complete the walk, and finish what I started. The journey has been tedious, long, heavy-hearted and uncomfortable, but never boring. I am grateful for what is real, this August month. I am learning to cope and to trust what is not. I leave the best bits to the imagination. There is so much beauty to be lived in between the cracks, and blazon, red iron will.

God is a mere mortal, off on some other planet. He can't save us. I can't save him. He sees me, us, he must? There are far too many coincidences amongst the living. I must forgive him, for forgetting and leaving me buried whole suffocating from the mud and the shit. There is plenty of time for dirty boxes, and bones, eternity waits. Bullshit, I say, burn me up in the woods with the leaves and the ants in bursts of fire engine red.

. . .

I walk the woods with a new friend; one who has chosen to come along. A funny, furry, marbled, and multi-color coated beauty.

She has traveled far, this fur ball baby, alone. Crossing oceans and deserts to come home. We have chosen this time together, this fleeting instant. The spirits had a hand in our reunion I've been told, aligning our stories in perfect sync. She is blind in one eye and I am disabled, but together we are whole. She puts her faith in me without reason. I watch her like a hawk, lovingly and cautiously loosening the reigns giving her space and freedom to explore, and to grow. We walk this waking dream in tandem, learning to navigate scary days.

I am in love all over again. With possibility, arrives a happier time than I remember. I will stay put on this planet for her, one reason to get better. She likes my woods and our walk. I wonder if she sees the off balance, oddball characters and friends I have made over the lengthy seasons, along the mad course. The subway man, shopping cart freak, parasol queen, kaleidoscope colors and Sadie lovely. She seems less inclined to notice my ghosts, and more inclined to bounce up to the blue people. I smile and look at the faces. It feels good to look up and stare less at the ground as we walk.

Sadie and this little wolf would get along. Perhaps Wolfie and I will make a trip to the beach come spring, something to look forward to. Dreaming is allowed on my planet and encouraged.

It costs not a thing. Ah but no, I have made a pact. We must finish the story soon before the sabbatical ends and time runs out. We have less than a hundred days to make sense of our time together.

I have not lost her completely, the gypsy in me. I have not yet forgotten the good parts, the quality person. I've managed to hold on to some of the noble parts, despite the self–obsessed, mortally wounded human.

I go back to the beginning when I grow dark, overwhelmed with madness. I offer everything to the sky, the outdated fashion, changing seasons, the fickle fame, the fancy shoes, and false living. I walk and walk, praying and cussing the heavens. I move forward until the blisters become thick and I can't feel the soles of my feet. I walk until the muscles soften, and the skin feels less prickly in the heat. Too sick to fret about overrated opinions, I let go of the jealous, judgmental person. I am too hard on myself, too quick to lose track, and too fast veer off course. I forget the little victories are the ones that count, they don't ask much and I never fall completely apart. I must stay the course, mind present and focused.

My beat up, weathered, backpack lays waiting, filled with the basic necessities to stay on track. She waits until I am strong enough to travel hanging out in a dusty room discarded, whispering my name. It's time to think about getting back to the blue planet, while the weather is mild and the mind permitting.

Nature has been very good to me, even in the throws of harsh seasons, demons, spellbinding frigid temperatures, wet rains, and manic, irrational moods. She has allowed me to continue. My legs are strong and able, I am mindful of that. One letter at a time, one word, one thought, one rapid cycle, one lasting memory, one sabbatical making sense of the absurd. Where visions of knives penetrating the skull seem less daunting, and blood cruising through the veins feels less agonizing. And where death is just another option to weigh in on. Or not.

· · ·

Where just this once, this one chance only cocooned in red bench security, from a nowhere town and a not so special existence, I get to call the last shot.

I type the type, moving the story in a different direction. My sweet wolf and I will head out to the beach, visiting my sleek, sexy, wall of glass beach home in all her splendid transparency. She will love it there, as much as I. Finding contentment in the solitude and sensory quietude on the shores of a vast magnificent coral, red reef. She and Sadie lovely will be sisters long lost, mirror images from different dimensions. I understand my head may be broken, but my heart is not. I have more than enough room in mind and spirit to love them both, together or apart.

Space-time travel and molecular, liquid-solid creatures have no mirrors and time has no clock.

THE SECOND HAND ESCAPE

Brandy at 2:00 o'clock on a splendid, sunny September afternoon is a welcome change, refreshing and renewing the air quality. She is here, my favorite month. We have few days left together before we reach our final destination. I include you reader, of course, who have been so gracious to come along. I've been blessed with flighty characters and peculiar, blue persons scattered along the course. I have leisurely wasted away the days, lingering perhaps in the fantasy, a wee bit too long. But the overzealous mind has allowed and indulged me so.

The truth? My everyday life consists of a walk. The rest is mundane living in abundance. Wake, eat, dress, walk, sleep, time and time again. The fight with my head to keep quiet, the bite of the tongue afraid of the inappropriate response. The shell of the person is all that remains. The successful other me is long forgotten, her dreams discarded and burned in a pile of crap.

I am petrified to look up. I hide out in my mother's house; the manic-depressive on edge, waiting to see which beast will rear its ugly head. I take the drugs; they don't help. They make me sick, spinning my brains squeezed tightly in a vice. I pick and pick, scratch and scratch at my unbearably, uncomfortable skin. I pace and pace and pace and pace. I talk to the air, praying for a reasonable response.

I want to crawl out of this mind-body until there is liquid nothing.

I am not winning this fight yet here I am, bored, deflated, and uninterested. And the noise, oh my god the unrelenting screaming thoughts, the noise squashes all else, reverberating the high-pitched, all-encompassing sound.

On most days when able, I place two feet on the floor, praying for the strength to just walk. A simple feat for most, walking for me is the small miracle. I don't care if I'm dead; the unhealthy parts leave me feeling helpless, ill thought. The fantasy moves ahead. Without my parasol queen, the homeless man and fabulous wall of glass beach sideways home, I am gone. I would not remain on this planet amongst the living, completely isolated. I would not hide off in a corner, head buried in shame, the lost lone alien, the ghost wandering aimlessly the blue planet.

I don't feel like the others, no longer wired the same. I am the nowhere drifter, the easy rider killing time, in search of the fast wave. Yet, I'm deathly afraid of the surf and being dragged under. Forty years of living, forty years of life is overkill at best. I know you must think me rude, ungrateful for the experience. That is only a half-truth. I have witnessed incredible beauty on this planet, despite my unsteady being. I have watched blue people do amazing things, perform kind gestures, make humble choices, and witnessed humane moments of sincerity.

. . .

I have been amazed and moved by these earthly beings and their majestic quality. I have laughed and cried and felt deep emotion, inspired by it all, the simplest of things. Sunsets, deserts, music, beaches and wide-open night ceilings twinkling the sky, all mouth dropping inspiring and second-hand minutes well worth living.

A half-century filled with rights and wrongs, irresponsible choices and a horribly misguided youth seem wasted. I'll stay here in my woods, for the time being, parked on a bench, the red safety zone. I'll mind my own business, keeping to myself. Dreaming liquid dreams and far away places, mystical oceans while basking in the silence, and anticipating the upcoming fall.

I want to go back for one minute. Travel a decade back in time, to a healthy, carefree, happier self. Where the labels on my back were less intimidating. The second-hand clock stops for no one, relentless and in perfect pitch. I delay the moment for a mere fraction, to relive it. The red robin flies exclusively for me. The gravel under my feet wakes me from a trance, gently coaxing me back to earth. To a place, I no longer recognize, so gravely misunderstood, to the disease that makes it so uncomfortable to be my friend.

Willard has closed her doors, the dark, cruel secrets and tortured insanity lies buried beneath the earth. The building remains, straight jackets hung up for good, unnecessary and out of fashion. There is no need for roughhousing the sick; the surly mind keeps one tightly wound, in a prison of their own making. The ghosts line the halls at night. Dancing and laughing after dark, set free in death to bask in the light.

My ancestors died behind those walls, awaiting their untimely fate, society's discarded hidden in secret, shame, and lies. Locked up and rejected by their own families, the locked away insane thrown out like rotting garbage. I have yet to be left in a square metal box to rust. I wait for the devil to deliver my death sentence. If you cannot bear to look at me, then don't. Turn away and face the wall. I completely understand. But pause perhaps, for a mere fraction of a second before acting in haste. The second hand still remembers the day I was whole and you were me, mocked and persecuted for not a single fault of my own.

The second-hand minute bears the weight of the time traveler, the life worth living and the one that is not.

GRAY MATTER

Today I was told I am to lose more and more gray matter, as the days go on. That is the natural brain course, the progression of things. Although I had guessed this was coming, the forgetful days, the angry frustration, the inability to navigate rapid cycling, panic, and despair, I had hoped it was not. I will lose more and more cognitive function as the disease and I move forward, greedily snatching sanity, the healthy mind parts. I work hard to remember; writing fast before the words escape me, and all that remains is an empty, fragile, sand dollar shell.

I watched a happy go lucky soldier full of my DNA, run the mind fields and lose the race. His ability to recognize the faces he adored, all gone. I helped on occasion, to change, wash and massage him, sprinkling lavender calm. I prayed he would be spared the long, cruel, mad journey, fueled by anxiety and fear. He would not want you to see it, the proud man who lived out his days helping others. He would not want to forget, bedridden, feeble, old, and waiting for death. Unable to recall the magnificent, strong, beautiful, bold person he had been. I watched as he gracefully and with ease drew his last breath; lifted up and away, out of the tormented mind and frail body towards the ether. No more pain, no more disease, no more lost memory. He became young again in an instant. In my eye's he was whole, able, and strong. That is God's greatest gift to the blue people planet, the ability to rewind and recall.

I am not that good. I am not that good a person. I am the selfish, head-racing lunatic desperate to find a way out, constantly in fear of her fate, and the bad luck hand I've been dealt.

My beach house is the necessary escape from harsh reality. I build parallel lives, alternate planets, parasol queens and white shiny things to get through the tedious task of living. To help navigate the course when the stars and sun no longer shine, when oblivion becomes the welcome respite.

I have little courage to walk. I don't want to lose the power of clear thought, the memories. I don't want to die alone, pitiful, homeless and forgotten. I don't want to live in puddle brain. I want grace, humility and the sweet scent of evergreen to fill the days and ease the nights. I don't know which blue person to trust, the scientists who say the foreboding dark is coming, or the friends and loved ones who assure me it is not. No matter about tomorrow, for today I must walk.

This September day is sent straight from the spirits, a beautiful, brisk, clear sky without a cloud above. The once in a lifetime Harvest moon and Jupiter beyond, brilliantly light the night. I have grown accustomed to noticing the little things, butterflies and fallen berries from the trees. I never thought myself fond of nature, preferring the beach or the electric, twinkling, city skyline. I have learned much about myself on the walk. I love these woods, her nurturing nature and the reassuring silence she has gifted me over these horrible, inevitable past months.

I am typing words, pausing for the brief second to reassemble the thoughts. I know my end is inevitable; gray matter gone missing reminds me the clock doesn't stops. I don't know exactly when which precise minute or thousandth day I'll be embers and ash, but I am grateful for the clarity today. My fingers find their way praying to a merciless God, begging for strength on the days that lie ahead.

I'm engulfed in a bubble and electric high voltage, casting a long shadow. I am fighting to tell the story, so that somewhere over vast oceans and arid desert, some unlucky bastard and their family find solace and kinship along the course. It's no longer interesting to hide behind the disease; she and I are in perfect symmetry melding into one. It's not fair to have to hide out, keeping up the façade that I am well. What's interesting is to have the raw courage to expose it, place it on the table, unashamed and unapologetic. The brain loses her way, so what, it happens. We're all waiting out fate. Human resistance is inevitable; the blue person thinks their life is all-important when in reality it is not.

It is the small matter at four percent and mere dust particles, in a universe far bigger than imagined, a trillion years complicated, questions left unanswered and ignored. Locked in the prison of the minds making life is simple; it's joy and suffering in tandem. One does not exist without the other.

Losing gray matter and the ability to remember is the sadistic, cruel, ultimate betrayal. I will have this story to look back on when I am old, gray and feeble minded. I will enjoy the tale, recalling a hint of the familiar, even when I don't recall taking the walk. It is highly personal, authentic, and the very best I could do. I tried hard to survive, not by society's cruel, ugly, stupid, moneymaking standards or judgments, but mine.

I could end it now. I could try to summon the courage to find a way to bury this planetary life. But, that would be selfish and untimely. I am here to fight. We live blind, in denial that time goes on forever, knowing full well it does not. I love the dark and its mysterious deviant ways, but I am in shock and awe at the power and beauty that is the light.

There are real people counting on me, to get better and grow strong. When I stop living in fear and breathe deeply, I am reminded of that.

I am blessed, and not yet forgotten. I am loved and that is enough to ignore the gray matter, dying parts.

PLEASE FORGIVE ME

I should've have stayed in. The rainfall has made the woods ominous, frightening and damp. A blue person sits comfortably perched on the bench. Oh no, what is he doing? Jesus fucking Christ, it can't be. He speaks as Wolfie races to greet him. Human niceties and simple conversation ensue, seemingly harmless enough.

Fuck, I should not have stopped. Suddenly, I am in fear for my life. Heart pounding, eyes twitching, shoulders and hands in a knot, I step up my gait. I can't talk myself out of the ridiculous notion and fear-driven pace. Unable to enjoy the walk, I wait for the blue person to pounce. My muscles tense, teeth ground to stubs.

I desperately try to move on, in spite of the brick weight feeling. The brutal attack plays out, over and over again. The bike lock cord tightens around my neck from behind, his dirty fingernails tearing my face. I resist, kicking and flailing my fists gasping for breath. It's no use. The somber, wet woods is my last walk, and gruesome, imminent end. Wolfie stays close to my corpse, quivering and whimpering at my side. The dark, gory images of dirt, blood and death, I can't shake them. All reasoning has vanished. I try hard to convince myself I am not dead, merely hyperventilating. Fucking paranoia sneaks in on an otherwise pleasant afternoon. How dare she? Despite my best, calming efforts, I pick up a rock. I place it in my pocket for protection, to bash in the skull of the menace lurking ahead.

Wolfie glances at me begging to run and play, I squash all attempts. I walk fast and heated, holding tight to the blunt object.

I want to flee these woods, my safe haven, screaming at the top of my lungs. Help! Someone please help me, I'm losing all senses. No one hears the screams; they are silent, decibels too high for mortal ears. I know how irrational, how crazy this seems. Not in my woods. I will not be tortured, not in this nowhere town, not from the bench where I call the shots, bringing crazy back down to manageable.

I will not die, though my brain tells me different. Not today, I will not. Tomorrow is hours, minutes and seconds closer. I will not be bullied, not on my sacred ground and not on this day, so close to a resolution. Every word counts this October month, the last chance at sanity. I bargain with the demons dancing in my head. How fitting Halloween marks the end of my calendar year and witches mark the anniversary, completing the pace.

I see red. Fall colors abound, my blood mixes with gravel and spit. My knees give out. I collapse, falling to the ground. I am helpless to reason with the out of control me. I take long, deep, healing breaths. It doesn't help. I am in full-blown, panic mode and cannot be calmed. Wolfie is scared and upset, still a puppy, she licks the fear from my face, soothing the inconsolable, shattered, unstable person, lying defeated on the ground. She doesn't leave or lose hope, she is persistent, and sticks like glue. Unlike the fickle, blue persons so quick to give up on others, to walk away from a difficult situation, hands thrown up in defeat.

I close my eyes, losing all reason. A silk glove caresses my cheek; I am instantly familiar with the light touch. The smell of lavender fills the air. She has come, my Victorian queen back from the ether to deal with the crisis. Invisible to all, she cannot speak, but her warm presence is felt all around me. She stays a long, long, while; we watch the sun go down together, one last time. The air starts to grow cold, a chill creeps over my bones. She sits quietly until the fear grip loosens its hold. Somehow, I feel better. The silent shrieking, ugly mess dissipates behind a black cloud, and I am homeward bound. The menacing, blue person has gone, back to his hearty hearth, doting wife and loving children. I was wrong.

I was so very, very wrong. He meant no harm, setting me off down a downward spiral.

Wolfie is calm and content. My parasol queen leaves one white glove behind, reminding me we are soul sisters requiring only half parts. I have an eerie, goose bump, funny kind of feeling; we will be forever separated and apart. The heavens, suns, moon, and parallel lives becoming the déjà vu memory. I do not bid her farewell, I simply cannot. She took extraordinary measures to be here. I don't mind the lingering empty. I carry her healing energy and elegance in my soul. Her regal essence and compassion embedded inside me, leaving me free to breathe again.

Oh no, no you don't. The greedy, icy blue planet does not win, breaking the red bench apart. I have struggled hard to let go of the superficial, unnecessary parts, learning to hold dear the important, jigsaw puzzle, pieces. Even in the midst of brutal mind rape, and unfair playing fields, do not feel sad. Puppy dog dreams must always win out.

My walkabout does not lie or paint an always pretty, white picket fence picture. She tells the truth on red October scary monster days, and bewitching, unexplained mystic wind whistling nights.

It's an odd, odd spectacularly bizarre thing this waking life. I am not sure how to navigate it, so I fuck up and live in the fantasy when afraid. I place my trust blindly on the page, letting the words guide me. I struggle to keep the faith, grateful for the few, brave individuals who share their space and time. The precious ones who care enough to still recognize my face, no matter how different it feels. They remind me constantly and with patience, I am the same beautiful, even atoms and molecules split apart.

They know none of this could be helped. It is the borrowed time, cruel fate I must bear with a heavy heart. Crazy does not discriminate and has taken up residence in my brain. The accusations, irrational outbursts, tears, depression, paranoia, anxiety, desperation, and crippling days, fill the pages. Where sunburst stars, teardrop lights and long ago, dead, waking queens take center stage, no matter how bizarre or impossible it might seem.

It's over-firing neurons at lightning speed and the overzealous, active imagination gone wild, apple bobbing at high velocity, simultaneously between dark and light.

It's exhausting and ruthless, this headspace. I will not lie; I am not a lucky person. But, I have been blessed with this one life. To fuck it up or fix it as best I can; as best as the shattered pieces allow.

And the beach, the reality and the dream are omnipresent. The mysterious, infinite immense ocean, sandy, easy days and red reef, tropical, fish seas make life worth living. Blue and turquoise neon ignite the water within, and the orange and pink horizon is the perfect backdrop for a God's gifted perfect day. I only need to close my eyes and I am there, magically transported to the mysterious, healing deep understanding how insignificant

I really am.

My neat, wall of glass beach home is filled with white, comfortable, cozy rooms, and wooden fixtures. It is me, naked, fucked-up and exposing my deepest thoughts naked in all my transparency as I tap into the imaginary corners of my mind, to mend the broken parts. Sadie love heals the hopelessness and isolation, and the beach helps survive the monotonous days and sleepless nights.

The stranger in my head, the dangerous blue man disappears. He was never a threat. How stupid to fall for irrational thinking, I know that now. Yet, the mind plays tricks and is ruthless. The poor bastard was content, ignorant and oblivious out for a bike ride. He couldn't care less about me. He's off living his own reality, far, far and away from my insanity.

I am liquid solid. It's hard to remember, to stay mindful of that. On the walkabout, I am atoms and molecules intact, one step ahead of danger lurking ahead.

HIGHFALUTIN SEQUINS & GLITTER

The weather is mild and pleasant from my place in the world, my red perch. The sunshine's bright; and the memories come alive dancing atop the reflections of the green water ponds. Showing me the past I did not ask to remember. But, perhaps I must travel back down that road before I can move forward. Because our days on the red bench are numbered, I must accept the past to paint the whole picture. It was a fabulous life me before insanity, the surreal way of living. The superficial, charmed life granted precious few.

I see a reflection floating along the crystal, clear water. The young girl, filled with so much promise; the tall, lean, freckle-faced, red-headed beauty. She seems so ugly, lost, foreign, forgotten and dead to me now. She is out of place in these nightmare days I am living. She was the gypsy, with golden luck illuminating her brazen, angel wings. She was bold, unafraid, and unapologetic along the road. The journey would be kind enough to grant her a taste of successful and sane living. Flitting off to Paris for fashion week working with the best of the best in fashion, Armani, Moschino and all the top designers was an ordinary day. Dining with celebrities was the perk of the life of a supermodel. People love hanging around the beautiful ones. It makes them feel better about themselves, even if the beautiful person is a facade and a rotten, stinking human being. The blue people don't care about the insides, more consumed with labels and stereotypes.

Billboards with my face plastered on them twenty feet above the streets of Milan seem silly and frivolous, distasteful to me now.

Exotic trips to far off places, Africa, Milan, Paris, London, Barcelona, Madrid, Hamburg, and Zurich, were taken on a whim. It was the luxurious life where beauty was the main attraction. Thousand dollar shoes lusted after, money spent in the blink of an eye. Never once considering what a thousand bucks would mean to a starving village, or my homeless man. With two cents in my pocket and waning pride, I get it now. Flights to Miami from Europe in the dead of winter just to avoid the bitter cold, and bask in the sun. Was that my life? It feels so off putting and far from me now.

Miami, the easy, breezy days, smoothies, beach, and the occasional job when I felt like working. Those were the best days; perhaps that is why I love a sideways beach. I lived the uncomplicated life, clocking the days on high tide time. I enjoyed the glamorous life a long, long time. I got away with being free and unaccountable, too young, irresponsible, and selfish to answer to anyone. I had dough, lots and lots of it. I had time, the greatest luxury of all. It was mindless and effortless. It felt like home, I was home. I didn't know any different.

If I had known what was coming up ahead, the hell I would be forced to endure, would I have shortened the trip, made better, smarter, more practical choices? I doubt it. We are so ignorant of time and wasters of so much energy. We are not the deciders of anything. It is all in the hands of a God I'm not even sure exists.

So, I'm guessing no. I would not have changed the past. I would have lived recklessly by the beach, the sea, the sun, moon, and stars for as long as possible. I would have stretched out the days, the gift of a heart, healthy mind in the company of people I loved.

And no, I can't go back to the glamorous beginnings, I can't even afford the ticket. I'm stuck here with this person who no longer resembles me; battling mind demons I can't control. I don't care, I am unafraid of death, or what comes next from this murky pond, perched on a red bench. I throw a stone into the water shattering apart the image and the optical illusion. She is not me, no more than I am her. I am glad the memory has gone and left me in peace. The birds are out singing; a macaw flies overhead in vibrant, curious, glorious color, wickedly out of place up north. Wolfie has grown impatient with my backward, reflective dance. She is puppy tail young, willing and eager to roam. She wants to wander, explore, and get on with it this thing called living.

The young girl dissolves inside the recesses of memory, and I am free to move on, letting go of the past and muddy waters. The beach house remains in the clear, calm wading pools of the mind and her beautiful, well-meaning imagery. The beach house is me, in all my raw, naked and brutal transparency shattering the walls and negativity holding me prisoner, unable to break free.

I must get moving I suppose, haunted by the past and future, overly cautious and wickedly sentimental. I must walk in the present, decked out in sequins and glitter in honor of the ballsy past. There is magic brewing in these woods and honest living inside the structured routine. Small town life is fine, filtering the air with H2O, and hyperbaric clean, 100% pure, brain oxygen.

. . .

Just when I think I am no more. I'm proven wrong. Just when I think I have absolutely nothing, to give, to fight, or to live. Not one day worth living. Just when there is not one breath left and my veins have dried up and turned purple. Just when there is nothing except black hole, bottomless tar pits, and green-eyed pond scum monsters, my dreams shake me from the hollows. My spirit guides dust me with just the right amount of determination while I sleep.

I awake unsettled yet refreshed by the pretty rainbow, mirror ball glow of sequins dancing across my ceiling. Pinching myself, the night fairies are the miracle enough to keep on living. Trembling,

I get on with the daunting task of getting up, out of bed, dressed, and greeting the new day.

Is it a dream? Did I imagine this? Which piece is the reality? Was I ever really here? Am I alive? Who can say? My dead don't speak to me now, so I can't be sure of anything. Where I came from or the direction I am heading. I can only sprinkle the earth with kindness, fondness, and grace learned over time and with age. The talking parrots fly above me now in bouts of beautiful memory and happy colors, are reminders that unexplained, mystical beauty remains.

Maybe, God gave me this curse on my head so that I would be forced to stop, slow down and to listen, taking in all the enchantment around me. I would not be this kind, sensitive, flawed, wildly imperfect or caring without the slightest touch of insanity. I would have stayed the small-minded, selfish, ignorant young girl never bothering to look up to take in her surroundings.

Never stopping to be here, right now. That is the only way I can justify the excruciating pain and suffering running through this broken brain and body. And the calm in knowing, that one day I will no longer be bound by the minutes, the blue planet a faded memory.

I will no longer be labeled the lunatic or crazy but will be ANANTA happy, safe and sound. I won't have to fight the spinning, dizzying head, the out of nowhere panic attacks leaving me doped up exhausted, or the unbearable despair pulsating my blood and my muscles. I will no longer silently scream inside from pain and anxiety, the spinner top raring to explode. I will be free to roam unencumbered by the weight of the world.

I thought if I went way back in time, to the glimpse of a young, healthy, jovial, carefree young woman floating effortlessly on the waters, you might take pity on me. One never knows which murky waters they find themselves thrashing about; life spares no one from suffering. The ripples shift and shape as they see fit, taking us all on our own personal journeys of hardship and grace. My struggle came a bit sooner than anticipated, leaving me grappling with a sickness I was ill prepared for. Still, I swim, float, and sink always paddling my way back to the surface for a breath and a bit of fresh air.

Clearing the cobwebs out of the way, I brace myself for the walk.

I make room for smooth take off and safe landing.

MOON DUST AND SPACE LANDING

I walk the blue planet, no grand plans laid out. I leave preconceived notions on the page, of how life should or should not be lived.

I walk, as best I can. I don't prepare for the future; I would not be so bold. I'm granted a two-second jump ahead, to see how it unfolds. An old lady hunched and defeated, I carry on stupidly with all my humanistic qualities, my pink parasol frayed and faded by the sun. I walk until my legs can no longer carry the weight of the exhausted mind, body. Tired and aged, they give out entirely. It's my time to say goodbye to the life I have known. In slow, dreamlike motion, I watch it pass by. I see the ones who truly loved me, their tender faces overcome with emotion.

It was a good life; it's time to say goodbye and move on. I was the blessed one. It was an honest live, full of love and compassion.

My blue planet people bid me farewell, tears welling up in their eyes.

They are horribly sad I must go, but I am teary-eyed and happy. Those who have gone before, wait excitedly with open arms, welcoming the cycle of death, and rebirth. They are here to guide me and help finish the story. I am liquid marshmallow, dissolving away bit by bit into nothingness, from an old woman's broken down, crooked body. I inhale one last breath releasing blue planet life and welcome the weightless feeling. I am different in this empty shell, more hopeful and freer than I've ever known. There is no pain in the ether, no sorrow, no joy, no valleys, no mountains, no highs and no lows. There are no mercurial moods, but only miles and miles of fireflies dancing. The light is so blinding I close my eyes to adjust to the new, transcendent surroundings. I feel my dead gently nudging me up and away, out of the aged body that was never meant to outlast the precious hours, days and minutes on earth.

I float. I no longer walk. I don't need the weight of my feet to keep me rooted to the ground, free falling towards the heavens. I look back one last time taking it all in, one final farewell.

Looking back, I marvel at the humans wasting time and energy, blue people mulling about worrying over nothing. Greed, ego, hate, injustice, lust and prideful emotions dissipate into vapors of dust. I watch compassion; generosity, kindness, love, humility and respect fall back to the ground. I ache a bit for the familiar. The silly, pagan rituals and ways, nostalgia washes over me.

I am brought back from my two-second glimpse of the future, less frightened and heavy. I make a solemn promise, vowing to live out my days, carrying the weight of this body with dignity and grace. By the simple movement of forward motion and the walk,

I aim for strong and healthy.

I don't let go of the madness but keep her close. She won't leave anyway, claws dug deep inside my brain. Even if I begged and pleaded for mercy, she would not go. She is my barometer, setting the tone for the day. She is the creative me, filling my world with a vivid, wild and dark imagination. She has shown me places and visions brighter and darker than ever imagined. However unwanted, she is a part of my identity. Without ever leaving the comfort of the page, she carries me off into the vast unknown. I am whisked off on a whim, without warning or notice, at the mercy of her whimsical, diabolic, multi-faceted ways.

Some days, I am consumed by the fear, spinning too fast, too high or too low, losing all control. Eventually the manic or depressive me, will burn out and explode. I let insanity take me, to places I have not known, to unexplained mystery, the abyss, and dark matter at the highest percent.

Despite my best efforts to loosen the vice grip, I give in and let go. Closing my eyes and preparing for takeoff, I unclasp my arms and unclench my fists. I grab onto the bench, and the one image that grounds me, a mother who won't let go. When I am lost in worlds I know not of and scared out of my mind I won't find my way back home, she soothes me. I have only to close my eyes, and hear her deep, steady voice of reason in the distance. Beckoning, she gently coaxes me home. She is rock solid, embedded in the folds of every corner of my mind, heart, and soul. She is here with me now, present, in her one-hundred-year-old home. The ever-constant presence, patiently waiting for my return, from worlds she can never know.

. . .

With one foot planted on the ground, and the other dancing with parasol queens and subway kings, I'm disappear whenever the mood suits. I'm not sure I can keep up this charade of good health. My mind is winning you see, disappearing each day into the void, gray matter dying bit by bit. I beg take it all so that I no longer remember the unnerving beauty here on earth. They tell me I must fight harder, but I don't see from where or how. The choice has never been up to me, no matter how heavy the armor I wear.

I am a shell of the old me, barely recognizing my own face. I have a soul, I'm sure. It feels pain, black abyss, and destitute sorrow. It finds joy in simple things when I can forget and get out of my head. The walking helps, it is the mindless task I can do without thinking too much. The writing keeps me grounded, and connected. I type in spite of the present insecurities of a futile, failed future looming ahead. If only the sun would come out, I might feel a glimmer of hope on a ray of sunshine.

Instead of despair on these sub-zero days, in parades of endless, tedious succession. I hate the color gray, the boring winter blank sky. I hate the cold, the incessant bitter freeze I can't shake. They say ECT may be the only way back, again, my mind resistant to the parade of drugs they shove down my throat. I don't care, zap my brain, shock it, and bring back some hope. Where is this God they talk so highly about? He's a slacker, watching over tsunamis, disease, dirty politics, and earthquakes swallow babies and their families whole. How could I think for one second he might take pity on me? When the rest of the blue planet has gone haywire. Killing for nothing, stealing, lying, cheating, concerned for number one. There is no honor and trust amongst new millennium thieves. We are a nation consumed with stuff, ego, and greed. Hey, look at me, how fabulous the façade. Maybe by spring, the hatred and contempt will be gone. Some warmth and compassion brought back into these cold-hearted bones. If I can just hang on until then, I might have a shot.

Things always seem brighter, warmer, kinder, and less drastic under the beautiful rays of a golden sun.

108 MARMAS

The levels have shifted again. Reason is demanding I listen. We have lived in the woods long enough. It's time to say goodbye to the visions and fantastical living. I have visited murky corners, shape-shifting dark into light. On the walk, the vibrational hum and healing meditation grant serenity, so the mind might even out.

I never trusted the path, stumbling and fighting my way along the course. I never trusted I was anything, the God loved person, carving a small space of her own. I never understood I couldn't control anything, stupid stubborn girl. I held on so tight, grasping at straws, consumed by terror and death. I forgot to honor the fearless, courageous, tapped into the bigger picture person, I had been. I forgot to follow her without question, into the woods, the bush, the bench, the carnival, the stars, parallel realities, the moon, and back. I continue the walk, curious to see how the life cycle plays out.

I'm not going back, to the pitiful, helpless, weak person. I found strength in others, good-willed and kind-hearted people who bothered to look up. I saw in their eyes, the belief that I mattered,

I let go of ego, for one delirious, fleeting second. I'm walking away from the past. I have different realities to face; where breath comes harder, and the lines on my aging face deepen, slowly melting away rough edges and rigid thinking.

I'm back on the bus. I thought I would die, to leave and venture out. Yet, here I am not dead. Autumn is upon us, in all her vivid splendor to greet me. The mind is sharp and in focus. The rustic, orange foliage and the burning bush are the vibrant colors I've not seen before. The woods, how different they look and feel. They are the perfect drug to gain perspective, transparent gold, rocky reds, and green-eyed mountains. Soothing the soul, they are the mishmash, fall melody.

We are at the end of our red hot, leisure days. Tomorrow is Halloween and marks the full year, a circular walkabout nearly completed. I am so very sad to leave the comfort of the page, but it is time to move on. Relearning how to get along with blue people and the planet, and finding some space to fit in. I am content for the first time in ages. It may not last more than this short-lived minute, but I'll take it, savoring the freedom and quiet.

I am grateful, lucky and blessed, after all. I am surrounded by love and acceptance. The mind disease didn't devour the soul; she leaves critical parts intact. She has not consumed my spirit. I am rock solid, this split second. I felt it; this thing called happiness, lived it on the skin, in my bones, dreamt it and willed it. I grasp the light particles of contentment. I am captivated, cocooned in a dream bubble, and molten liquid fairy tale.

. . .

I will not kill off fantasy and the beautiful characters that have crossed my path. They are me, I am them. We walk this waking dream, together. I revisit my shopping cart lady when lost and in need of a reality check. I dive into the dark, depths of emotion and relate to subway man, to the unnerving compassion felt for the homeless adrift. I revisit his reality from time to time so I won't forget. I remember far too well his miserable, sorry state. I co-habituate his unlucky circumstance, messed up and tangled inside misfired neurons and brain muscle.

My Victorian, parasol queen with the long, cascading, golden curls dons' crinoline and lace. She lives in another dimension, buried deep within the molecules and memory. Every so often, when I'm scared or feeling blue, I put on sateen, caressing and consoling my face. I revel in the healing, Victorian touch, and possibility. I rediscover empathy, treading lightly when dealing with the fragile, weird, crazy, off-putting ways of the blue people.

I save a spot for everyone on my bench, those afraid, confused, or in need of a safe, neutral territory. I take a stake, and drive it through the heart of disease, killing off this final piece of the puzzle. Fuck off and go away, chemical imbalance. I am not giving in, or giving up. I am not quitting. I am molecules and energy alive, chakras realigned, dashes in balance, spitfire and spirit fighting to loosen the reigns, slowing down the pace and ignoring box living.

I want a life filled to the brim, with messy colors, belly laughter and emotion, never lacking in serenity, understanding, calm, and a cool, headspace.

. . .

I take excellent care of my fantastic, beach home by the sea, readily accessing the sideways life whenever necessary. I grow bougainvillea, magnolia, jasmine, and lush floral gardens to breathe in the bouquet of color. I keep a quiet, clean, comfortable, Zen home, filled with ancient Sanskrit writing, and wide open, white spaces. I write, work, eat, rest and play. I regenerate the mind and body deep in meditation, to create. The ocean, her magic powers, and mist are very real for me. I understand the dark, deep blue depths of her waters flowing through me, and her buoyant, freedom qualities. I have been enthralled with the sea, lived near the ocean. It is the easy, accessible memory, where all that I love is safe, and securely in place. The Dolphins dance gracefully, blindly familiar with the exact rhythm of the waves and the surf. They are stoic creatures, in tune with the mysterious, ancient ties to the deep. I take comfort in their eloquent, natural rhythm, emulating the dance.

My Sadie love and I are happiest by the sea, free to run and roam as we please, finding our way back home instinctively. There is no job, no silly rules, no societal pre-conditions. There are no blue people filling our heads with insecurity. There is no timetable, no clocks on the walls to micromanage the days. We wake at dawn by the sun and live basic, never overextending our reach.

Much like our ancestors who existed in perfect pitch with the earth's rhythms, moon, sun, stars, and sea. Sadie is loved, adored and admired, greatly by me. I am grateful for our space-time travel, creating the perfect life off in the dream state. The vision is sacred, it is me intact at my very best, the creative person pure and open, living out her dharma, in her magical kingdom. The vision keeps me moving forward, towards the sea, planting the seeds, meticulously gathering tools cultivating balance.

The sideways, mind fuck of a life morphs effortlessly into reality.

. . .

Wolfie is a new reality, a critical part of the walkabout, and circular journey. I waited years and many lifetimes for her to come. I knew the second she arrived; the déjà vu feeling confirmed the now moment was ours to share. She showed me a way back to the enormous depth and space of my heart. I forget my plight, the sick, damaged person, the dizzying vortex, and out of control spiral I am. I find happy hanging out with the fuzzy, warm, sweet, furball of unconditional love and contentment. She gets me out of my head, and the dark, obsessive, world of mad uncertainties. She greets me with puppy breath and warm kisses.

I'm ok today, and that is a bold statement. I have real responsibility and a lovely shadow. As for the blue people, I must try my best to get along, be less harsh, pass less judgment, and shrug off their foreign ways. I will try to understand their stories and perhaps learn a lesson. I leave behind the superficial, the stuff and the shoes because it's hardly worth the weight. I saw a glimpse of something better, something bigger than me. I can't go back to the shadow life. The superficial stuff no longer fits in my duffle. I must pick and choose carefully the pieces and purpose it contains.

I dedicate my walkabout, my life and my imperfect, blue being qualities to those that have walked this year alongside me. They never judged, never ran from the hard, strange, shell of a person. They never saw me diseased. They cared for the shattered bits expertly, and mended them, meticulously with grace and kindness.

To the mother who fought for her child, I owe her all that I am, her kindness, compassion, strength, and warmth sustains me. She lovingly soldiered on, illuminating my way back from insanity, no matter how heavy the price. When I was screaming I hate you, talking nonsense, locked up in a psych ward for a month, shouting obscenities, conversing with the dead, getting rounds of shock treatments, Haldol shots, Benzos, Lithium, and Seroquel to even out, she fought for me. When I was hallucinating off in some other world she visited and sat by my side, uncertain the madness would release me back to her. Not knowing if I'd gone too far over the edge, she advocated when I could not. She never gave up, even when I did, promising I would come home again. And, I would.

I would never be the same, there would be years spent paralyzed, afraid to venture out, betrayed by my own mind. I was barely alive and it would take a long, long, excruciating while before I felt some semblance of myself. But not her, no. She saw me, her daughter all along. Perhaps she lied and told me what I needed to hear, to heal and recover. She is not a blue person at all but has red hot, boiling blood cruising her veins. There is no shadow of a doubt that I have been loved, and worth fighting for. I am not lucky by nature but blessed to be have been seen and cared for. That is all this manic-depressive blue person could ever dare hope for. The rest is just stuffing, lining the days.

I will not abandon my woods, my dreams, my life, the beach or the walk. I will continue, for as long as God wants and allows. I am liquid solid, someday I will return to the sublime, free-floating, nothingness state. Until then, I lovingly pack a bag filled with pages of stories, my most favorite memories, heartaches, and unbearable burdens. I will bury it deep inside the earth's magic, wishing well. Hoping someday in a long away, distant future, these stories might help another young anthropologist digging deep in search.

I was never alone on my quest for purpose, peace or happiness.

There have been others along the route, suffering in silence, from some madness or another.

The red bench. I love the red bench. I honor the comfort she holds, the portals opened, and the sacred space shared, day after glorious, monotone day. The red bench stays put for the rest of my days, however many thousands of minutes left, to finish the walk. I carry her iron will and fortitude deep in my gut, hoping to live out this blue person life with grace and gratitude, in peaceful co-existence.

I don't know how to say goodbye to the page. That is the hardest part; leaving the safety net I have grown accustomed to. So attached to the words and the characters, no longer sure if I am them or they are me. I thank God and the spirit guides, who have not always been friends, but great nemesis' in times of confusion and sorrow. I thank them for letting me vent, doubt, rant, and rave, posing the serious questions. I thank the planets, stars and alternate realities for not taking it seriously, showing me infinite possibilities and the strength to go on. The minutes of clarity and the opportunity to walk unencumbered on the open road, clearing the way for the gypsy and the time traveler, one small step at a time.

The pixie dust floats freely now, sprinkling the air with golden specks of light. Love, real in your face love, never loses hope. It defies all logic, transcending illness, magic, planets, time and infinity. I'm sprinkling the air with pixie dust, love, and childlike qualities so that we might grasp wonder in these shaky, fast times of uncertainty.

The walkabout, the sabbatical and I have come to terms with the unbearable, inexplicable, intricate workings of the mind. I'm accepting the law of least effort, embracing the unknown and my fate, with a wide-open heart. I have assembled the tools and the pitter-patter of the tap. Imperfection, panic, disease and all, I am choosing to walk.

I am worthy of living this one life. I am worthy of loving deeply. I am worthy of being loved, broken and put back together.

RADICAL ACCEPTANCE

On this gloomy, wet, Halloween afternoon leaves pile high concealing the grass, as a slight mist of my tears fills the air. I must say goodbye and thank you for the moments. For the three hundred and sixty-five hundreds of days spent with the lost soul in search of a purpose.

I look back on the road with no regret, humbled and in awe of where I have been, and the horrible days lived. I look cautiously towards the future with trepidation, anticipation, and hope. I would want no other me, no other life. I walk the path alone, without the ghosts and fantasy. Just a girl, a simpleton, beat up and worn down by a mind she can't control, dancing jazzy blue.

I do not care about minor details; I'm counting on the bigger picture. I'm counting on God, faith and the blue people to see me through. My puppy and I wander aimlessly and free, the future mapped out by the gravel laid down before us. I bask in simplicity. A drop of golden, yellow sun warms my pant leg as I sit on the bench, thinking about nothing. Thinking about nothing at all, except how good the heat feels. The gap poetic and blissfully quiet, I have worked hard to discover. I am present. I am here; here I am. The red bench and I molded into liquid steel, solidly glued back together.

Tomorrow will come, or it won't. I needn't remind myself of that. I mustn't worry about the minutiae. I have only to concentrate on the walk, making the now minutes count. I carve my name into my bench for posterity so that I might never, ever forget how sick I have been. I take a small chip of loose paint and place it on my tongue, swallowing it whole. Wherever I go, wherever I am, however good or bad the days I carry the strength of red bench inside me. The red bench will always be the guardian of my secrets, the keeper of the best and worst most intimate parts of me. Long after the walk and I have gone, a million miles far and away from the blue people and her planet the red bench lives on.

A precious little girl, with ringlets and golden hair wearing velvet and lace from a far off future, sits on my bench. Enjoying the pretty, brand new spring day. Innocent and free from worry, she squeals and claps her hands with glee, watching her puppy run and play. Just like I did, so many lifetimes ago. The red bench whispers in her ear my most important secrets, giving her all the wisdom and tools she will need to live out her days happy, and carefree.

I hope the world she lives in is a kinder place to dwell. I pray the blue people have learned compassion towards the disabled, the weak, and the mind sick. I hope that time has made her world a softer, more humane place to visit. Where race, judgment, shame, and fear have been obliterated from her planet, coloring her life with only jovial minutes. She will grow up to be a robust woman, a great healer, fearless traveler, headstrong warrior and the gypsy traveling the globe healing the sick. She is me the dreamer, only better, the direct descendant of all that I was not. She will do everything I had hoped to accomplish in life and more. She will not fall short, cut down by a disease more complicated than life itself. She will grow up brave and strong, a clearheaded and fine woman. I get to watch, dust particles in heaven floating over her head. We have come full circle, my friends. Only in death did I understand my limitations never mattered, and disease didn't win. The spirit guides that came before tried to show me the easier, less complicated route. I should have paid better attention when I was alive. I should've have listened, but I was all wrapped up in my head.

I will protect my golden ringlet girl, guiding her ever so gently from the heavens, sheltering her from the storms. My death never mattered one bit, only the courage, grace, and strength of how I lived carries on. In the face of adversity, I hope I am remembered as kind, loving and hating myself in real time.

ABOUT THE AUTHOR

Jacqueline Cioffa was an international model for 17 years and celebrity makeup artist. She is a dog lover, crystal collector, and Stone Crab enthusiast. Author of the poignant soul-stirring saga, "The Vast Landscape" and "Georgia Pine," Jacqueline's work has also been widely featured in numerous literary magazines, and anthologies. She's a storyteller, observer, truth teller, essayist, potty mouth, beauty enthusiast and film lover who's traveled the world. Living with Manic Depression, she believes passionately in using her voice to advocate and inspire others.

Author Site: jacquelinecioffa.com.

Her soul-stirring saga THE VAST LANDSCAPE, and GEORGIA PINE is available on Amazon.com.

ABOUT THE AUTHOR

ACKNOWLEDGMENTS

I'd like to thank my mother, Ellen May Hickey Cioffa for knowing precisely when to push and when to pull. She is the one, stable and loving voice in my head. To my brother, Tom, for being the most insightful creative person I know. Jack and Terry Hickey, thank you for giving birth to the most magnificent, brilliant daughter. Her exemplary life gives my life meaning, and the desire to use my voice to make a difference for those struggling with mental illness. To my father for his love and guiding light, you were a king among men. Without him, I would not have experienced the meaning of profound love.

Kara Moran, thank you for challenging me to push a little bit farther, for every single adventure and for never giving up during the darkest, craziest days. Malena Holcomb, thank you for being the sister of my soul, the early reader, and encourager of every word, and the keeper of my secrets. Gianni Ghidini, thank you for your keen observations on art and teaching me to always dig deeper.

To Sue Cioffa and the girls. Thank you for being omnipresent, no matter my mood or the weather.

My gratitude for their early and forever support goes to Julie Davidow, Felice Pappas, Patricia and Giuseppe Piazzi, Tim Quinn, Suzanne Hai, Dr. Parker, Patricia Nash, ILIV staff, Julie Anderson, Patrizia Ferrante, Mark Blickley, Rachel Thompson, Rebecca Batties, Ken Metz and the tireless mental health advocates raising awareness.

Thanks to Lupita, my furball shadow who loves me colorblind.

Dr. Laurie Beth Hickey, your extraordinary life cut short makes me more determined to live with grace in spite of this bastard mental illness. When I am lost in the minefields of paranoia, fear and raging battles with the mind your smile and spirit guide my way. You more than anyone I have ever known loved being alive.

NATIONAL SUICIDE PREVENTION LIFELINE

Call 1-800-273-8255

Suicide prevention and mental illness need to be talked about openly, just like any other disease. It is a beast with tentacles attached inside the deepest crevices of the brain.

To anyone living with mental illness, you deserve a goddamn medal. I feel you. I understand and respect your courage. To anyone loving someone with mental illness, I feel you and I understand your frustration and pain.

It's a mystery even to me, after two decades.

Be kind and generous with your time, and be patient with things we can't understand.

You might very well save a life today.

To the orbs and the power of a beautiful chaotic mind, I thank you for all the mind-blowing colors and feelings that obliterate the dark days.

Heed the ghostly whispers whistling on the wind
Hush now
It's perfectly fine to hang onto the memories
But it's high time to let go
You human are doing just fine on your own
Besides
There are 777 lifetimes between us
Sometimes separate and others bound too tight together
Making it hard to distinguish where one life ends and another begins
Never forget
I have loved you
I have loved you so
I have been loved so well, my ghosts
For that I thank you
Cherishing our time together in the here and now
Go ahead and move on
I understand
I am alive without you
Beyond the ether, I cannot go

Made in the USA
Middletown, DE
21 May 2019